ALL JOIN HANDS

THE FORGOTTEN ART OF PLAYING WITH CHILDREN

HEIDI HARTWIGER

ILLUSTRATED BY SUSAN TRACY

DOWN HOME   Down Home Press, Asheboro, N.C.

First Printing, September, 1994
9 8 7 6 5 4 3 2

ISBN 1-878086-32-4

Library of Congress Catalog Card Number
94-068508

Printed in the United States of America

Cover and book illustrations: Susan Tracy
Book design: Elizabeth House

Down Home Press
P.O. Box 4126
Asheboro, North Carolina 27204

There Was A Child Went Forth

There was a child went forth every day,
And the first object he look'd upon, that object he became,
And that object became a part of him for the day or a cer-
tain part of the day,
Or for many years or stretching cycles of years.

Walt Whitman

This book is dedicated to my children

Chris, Jenny, Matt, and Sandy Hartwiger

and to

Joel Bland, Kathy Ahern Hartwiger,
Jon Leeds, and Tiana Perry,

who seem like my children

A special thank you goes to Tamara Baxter, Linda and Donna Grant, Butch, Irene and Kellie Holder, Bette Hughes, Jane Krause, Dot Jackson, Martha Macdonald, Charlotte Ross, David and John Stuppy, Isabel Zuber, the ever-patient and resourceful faculty, staff and students of York High School, my SELU Sisters, and dear friends in the Appalachian Writers Association who shared their joys of childhood with me.

Contents

Introduction

Schedules! Deadlines! From a Robert Frost perspective, too many miles, too many promises before sleep. Prioritize your agenda, and who must wait? Who sits alone, looking very small, eating dinner in front of the television set? Who goes to sleep propped up in bed with the light on waiting for you to get home from a power dinner? Who roams the mall or is dropped at the movies while you run errands? Is this your child?

If you tire of constant rushing, does it matter? You meet this obligation, accept that responsibility, do what must be done to "better" your way of life. Things get complicated, and there aren't enough hours in the day.

Have you spread yourself so thin that you have no reserve energy? Is creativity a dot on the horizon? Then, how must children and young people feel? During school, while participating in sports, when scheduled for the "best enrichment activities ever", they are told to "plug in", to "make the connection."

What is missing from this picture is "unplugged" time – a time with no thoughts of tests or criticism, success or loss.

My life among children, my own and those I teach, has led me on a curious and wonderful journey. They perceive me as accepting and nonjudgmental and so allow me into their celebrations of discovery, their mourning for things lost.

Lately, the scales have tipped, weighing heavily on things lost. Relationships, traditions, and sense of personal identity struggle while isolation steps to center stage. I am impatient with those content to wring hands and profess concern for young people yet say there is nothing that can be done. Although I would like to take on the world in my campaign to return childhood to its rightful owners – the children, I haven't the resources for the solo undertaking. But I can, as you can, work one day at a time reaching one child at a time, knowing this makes a difference.

Because I believe playing with children is a forgotten art, I have collected from friends and practical experience some time-honored, surprisingly simple yet fast-fading and often overlooked ideas that I hope will help you rejuvenate your creative energy. Go ahead, dust off some family traditions lost in the attic of time, and revive the forgotten simplicity of having a good time. Follow your natural rhythm!

One of Henry David Thoreau's conclusions after his sojourn in the woods by Walden Pond was not to worry when out of pace with those around him. Do you hear that different drummer? Encourage your "self" and children around you to break rank, slow down, free up the five senses, discover and enjoy a wonderful world! Here and there a little Transcendental wisdom is good. As Ralph Waldo Emerson observed in his essay, *Nature*: "The sun illuminates only the eye of the man but shines into the eye and the heart of a child."

Quite possibly as you gear down activities, positive thoughts and small but special events rediscovered will be sun in your heart. Consider the change as moving from activating a hi-tech no-handle faucet to priming the squeaky, creaky old outdoor hand pump. It is tough at first. Pump the handle up and down, up and down and eventually the cold refreshing water flows.

Children thrive on simplicity. Hearing and rehearing, telling and retelling anecdotes creates a sense of personal history which is reassuring security to a child, especially in teen years when spirit, mind and body are not always in sync. Even as adults we enjoy a certain comfort zone in our own personal history. And there is no price tag on sharing such simple things.

Once upon a summer day, seated on a wooden swing in a weeping willow tree, a little princess waited, wiggling her bare toes in the filtered sunlight. She expected Prince Charming at any moment to burst through the bayberry hedge with bread and butter and sugar sandwiches. I was that backyard princess with trees, flowers, and hedges as my domain. My transient subjects, frogs and bugs, birds and butterflies were sources of great entertainment. Frequently Mark, the neighbor prince and his little sister Mary Kaye, did indeed come through the hedge with great provisions. From their kingdom down the road my friends brought soft store-bought white bread, spread thick with butter and plenty of sugar. We pressed thumb prints into the fold-over sandwiches. At the conclusion of each royal feast, we took long drinks of icy cold water from the pump, probably creating dough balls in our stomachs. We survived.

Even now, from time to time if I see soft margarine on the kitchen counter near the sugar bowl, I'll dip the tip of my finger into the margarine, into the sugar, then into my mouth. At that gritty sweet moment, I am the backyard princess.

Chances are as you read this, you already have a sugar story coming to mind that takes you back. Didn't you have a brother or sister who tried to stir two inches of sugar into a glass of iced tea? What about unexpectedly skating around on the kitchen floor gritty with sugar spilled during cookie baking? Or your forearm bonding to the plastic tablecloth after sugaring your oatmeal?

The point is neither to promote sugar consumption nor keep the neighborhood dentist in business, but rather to illustrate how by glimpsing a bit of my "personal history," a fond memory returns to you.

As we constantly press forward, nomads searching for the focus that will lead to meaningful relationships, experiences and goals, we lose something. An old friend in West Virginia once was introduced to a newcomer and addressed the stranger in this manner: "So here's where you live, but where are you from?" You know your address dear reader, but do you recall where are you from? This is not a geographical question, no maps needed. Rather this addresses the heart. Start priming the pump.

Writers, musicians, philosophers and all sorts of people experience the inborn, unmistakable urge to return home. This passion will nudge, push, then finally propel. From Dvorak's traditional *Going Home* melody that runs through his *From The New World* Symphony to The Grateful Dead's sweet sad "going home" words in *Broke Down Palace*, the idea of going home is cross-culturally pervasive.

Get comfortable with the desire to return to your home, your focus. It's not because you wish to be a child again or even to relive childhood; the desire is to reaffirm who you are – not what you do, how you dress, or where you live. Perhaps something will trigger one of your senses: wood smoke, a turkey roasting, children laughing in the late afternoon, a siren, a dog barking, wet shoes and for a fleeting moment, you'll be back to your center, your home.

Each spring for three years now a pair of robins has returned to my backyard world of dogs, lawnmowers and summer downpours. I've watched this couple nesting in the ligustrum hedge, hatching, feeding and launching their fledglings. Not until their mission is complete do they take off to winter quarters. What distinguishes their home hedge from other hedges? What is the inner drive that pushes a robin or person to complete the circle and return home?

When I was a fledgling, my grandmother, the one I called "More Momma," nudged me, encouraged me to try my wings, expand my farm girl horizons without losing my way home in the process. "Look over your shoulder, and as long as you can see the homeplace, you'll never be lost," were her words that long ago would send me out to play.

In those days I stretched my boundaries to the limits as I hiked through the cow pasture up to the small farm pond. Even when the woods were thick, in full leaf, I knew I was fine. From my vantage point by the pond I could see the clothes on the line, the corner of the house, the tip of the chimney. In full view of God, our cows and More Momma, I played by the pond, conjuring excitement. What if gypsies kidnapped me as they passed – as I knew they would – through Frog Hollow? Oh, joy!

On occasion More Momma's words return to me, as I watch the backyard flying school, when I hear the birds sing before daybreak, as the mosquitoes bite me in the garden, in the wind at sunset. It has not always been that way. As my version of the old saying goes, "I got the girl out of West Virginia, but try as I might, I couldn't get West Virginia out of the girl." For a large portion of my adult life I moved forward, neglecting to look over my shoulder until the homeplace diminished to a dot in my mind's eye. As I became engulfed by "the musts and have to's" in the process of daily living, I began to lose my center, the perspectives, the ideas, the truths important to me.

The English Romantic poet William Wordsworth must have known the sorrow of being caught up and tossed about in life without savoring the essence of living. The following four lines open his sonnet, *The World is Too Much With Us*:

The world is too much with us; late and soon,
Getting and spending, we lay waste our powers:
Little we see in nature that is ours;
We have given our hearts away, a sordid boon!

Do you have a growing dread as you pick up the morning paper or listen to the evening news? Without fail, there is the tragic litany of human problems. While most of us have the good fortune to know vivacious, happily adjusted children and teens, we also see troubling signs among the young people. One of the most unsettling is a growing lack of concern about anything except personal gain and instant gratification.

This trend knows no economic or geographic boundaries. It could be fueled unknowingly by hardworking, well-meaning, over-compensating, over-indulging parents who try positive but inconsistent discipline or material rewards to extract a certain level of behavior. Others apply restriction after restriction, or as an extreme measure resort to medication to effect change.

The family unit may function more like a household of strangers with no sure friend for a young one in distress; these days it is a rare home that has a grandparent or auntie in residence to be a confidant when "nobody cares." And who then keeps the family traditions going?

Plenty of time for video games, no time for family stories. There is also the false notion that the peculiar partnership of microwave foods and organized sports insures nourished, active bodies. The caution light blinks virtually unnoticed; nevertheless, people question how we were detoured onto such a rutty road.

There is hope! Remember the story of "Pandora and The Golden Box?" The lovely mythological maiden's world was a wonderful place free from all ills and sorrows. When given the beautiful box, Pandora was instructed that under no circumstances should she open it. Of course curiosity got the best of her; she decided to steal just one little peek. As the lid creaked open, there was a rushing sound, and all terrible things, pestilence, sickness, greed and ugliness were released into the world. By the time she snapped the lid shut, hope was all that remained.

As long as the sun rises and the seasons change, we have the opportunity to change the way we do things. Deep within, dear reader, you know you have that homeplace of which I speak. With that realization comes a mission. Help the young or young in spirit around you to locate, love, and respect their homeplaces too.

I cannot emphasize enough, as you consider the suggestions in the following sections, that you keep in mind you can make a difference. Use this as an idea book, a springboard to your own creativity. Temper your activities with laughter, simplicity, and flexibility. Wordsworth's idea that "the child is the father of the man" may be expanded, pointing to the idea that today's activities are tomorrow's fond memories which in turn provide the sign posts directing us back home. The following suggestions should help you at least get the shoelaces tied and so to set out on the right foot for your odyssey:

Always:

1. Be flexible. Have plan A, B. and C if necessary. If the unexpected interrupts the plan, go with the new opportunity.

2. Keep it simple, relaxed, and pleasant!

3. Let learning be a natural by-product of the experience, not the driving force.

Never:

1. Quiz, drill or require recitation of experience to others.

No "yes...buts!" You can do it. Have you ever been in a crowd and looked up appearing to see something, and the rest of the people followed your gaze and looked up too? If you haven't tried it, do. If you've experienced it, then you've had the first lesson in simple fun!

For some momentum, turn again to William Wordsworth. Consider his advice about putting away books for a while in order to learn from Nature:

The Tables Turned

Up! up my Friend, and quit your books;
Or surely you'll grow double:
Up! up! my Friend, and clear your looks;
Why all this toil and trouble?

The sun above the mountain's head,
A freshening lustre mellow
Through all the long green fields has spread,
His first sweet evening yellow.

Books! 'tis a dull and endless strife:
Come, hear the woodland linnet,
How sweet his music! on my life,
There's more of wisdom in it.

And hark! how blithe the throstle sings!
He, too, is no mean preacher:
Come forth into the light of things,
Let Nature be your teacher.

She has a world of ready wealth,
Our minds and hearts to bless-
Spontaneous wisdom breathed by health,
Truth breathed by cheerfulness.

One impulse from a vernal wood
*   May teach you more of man,*
Of moral evil and of good,
*   Than all the sages can.*

Sweet is the lore which Nature brings;
*   Our meddling intellect*
Mis-shapes the beauteous forms of things:-
*   We murder to dissect.*

Enough of Science and of Art;
*   Close up those barren leaves;*
Come forth, and bring with you a heart
*   That watches and receives.*

William Wordsworth

Traditional Games

Much about life in our time suggests that we have become pilgrims in an alien land; it seems we are always on the move, relentlessly searching to "find" and "empower" ourselves.

Consider the dollars exchanged for self-help books, for "getting in touch" with one's inner being, or for this or that self-therapy, and "feel good" courses. Why has such an appetite developed for these things?

Certainly introspection has its place. Yet as folks turned inward, seeking personal fulfillment, "liberating themselves," it appears that people-to-people communication suffered and finally slipped beneath the horizon.

The portable – sometimes disintegrating – family emerged. The live-in Granny, Grandpa, and maiden Auntie who were available for conversation and consolation, who knew how to change sheets on a bed with a sick person still in it, who shared fine humor and succinct wisdom from living many years were no longer partners in the household.

Tiny radios and portable cassette players with headphones moved the isolation process along nicely. Mega channel cable television appeared, and VCRs offered the opportunity to slouch in a chair mesmerized, watching the same tape over and over. Now computers offer an educational jump-start for toddlers and for others, instant information gratification when connected to a computer network.

And, as we lose the art of verbal communication, we are literally and figuratively losing touch with physical communication.

It is the natural order of things for both humans and animals that the young challenge the elders. When my soon-to-be husband took me to his home for that first family introduction, to his surprise he found his little brother had grown taller than he. The unspoken challenge was there, and it was settled by a wrestling match in the back yard. Sure enough, the torch was passed and little brother was victorious.

I recall my own three brothers' rites of passage to manhood, their wrestling matches in the living room with Dad that ended when eventually he had to say "Uncle!" or "I give!" as my mother always scolded, "The living room is not a gymnasium!"

I watched the same ritual performed by my own sons and their father. And yes, more than a thousand times I know I have repeated my mother's "gymnasium" words. In turn, as each one has "bested Dad" the mutual respect has deepened. Now my sons are older, and much to my husband's relief, they have followed my brothers' examples and turned to arm wrestling. To this day at family gatherings, father to son, brother to brother, uncle to nephew, the "besting" challenge continues.

Why would a child choose the companionship of an electronic beep over the company of a real live friend? Except for a power outage or dead batteries the technological friend won't let you down – or demand very much, either. Real friends are risky because relationships require personal communication, not video interaction. Also, real friends can't be turned off with a palm-held zapper. Or changed at will.

Is it possible that the electronically-isolated child has forgotten how to play – or simply never ever learned?

Periodically, it is suggested by politicians that we "re-invent government." Educators spur us on to "re-invent" education. Is there a need to "re-invent" fun?

Why not dust off some of the games that have moved far back in our memories? When I am with a group of people waiting in a check-out line somewhere, in the stands at a soccer or hockey game, or in the passenger area waiting for an overdue airplane, I like to try to work the topic around to "what we did when we were kids." Initially I get small frowns, vague memories. Then the big smile. "We used to...." And strangers on the periphery join the conversation.

Betsy Turner, who through the years taught all my children Latin and is now a colleague, hailed me from the far end of our high school's main hall. "I talked to my dad last night, and he reminded me about Bongo Board! That's what we called it – Bongo Board!" Her smile was triumphant as she recalled Bongo Boarding times with her brother at their childhood home in New York State.

Not only did her enthusiasm bring me joy and fond memories of our West Virginia version of a similar balancing game; it brought me also an inner satisfaction that she and her father found enjoyment in a shared family memory.

As a result of Betsy's conversation with her dad, the Turner children, Robert and Sarah, are acquainted with the almost forgotten art of Bongo Boarding. And so it is passed to yet another generation.

For several years during hockey season, faithful Hampton Roads Admirals hockey fans Butch and Irene Holder have sat behind me. When asked what she enjoyed playing as a girl, Irene was hesitant, then laughed about throwing a ball over the roof or bouncing it off the roof. Her gentle enthusiasm was contagious as she discussed the finer points of Jacks, and finally confessed to her favorite game, another ball bouncing game called Seven Up.

Listening, Butch sat quietly until we were finished. Then he said, "Marbles, that was my game." With a broad grin and an unmistakable twinkle in his eyes he lost the tired frown of a man who'd worked too many long hours.

Butch's pleasure brought to mind how many a day I stood in awe and amazement, looking at my grandfather's jar of glass marbles. On special occasions, Sunday afternoons or when I was sick in bed, my grandfather took the marbles from their sanctuary. One by one he held them in the hollow of his hand for me to see. He would roll these old friends between his fingers and tell me stories of these wondrous glass treasures.

He seemed especially fond of two large marbles, the shooters. He had names and stories for the small marbles, too. One he called a "cat's eye" and showed me the wave of color that ran through it that

3

caused it to indeed resemble a cat's eye. A cloudy one with thin pink stripes he called peppermint. The multicolor one was his "rainbow." A glass marble purist, my grandfather shunned the steelies, marbles not of glass but of shiny metal resembling ball bearings.

With his marble stories he held me, along with the marbles, in the palm of his hand.

Go ahead! Strike the match to rekindle your memory, starting with suggestions from this section. But don't settle for a spark. Fan the flames. Light the torch and smile at people. Talk to them. Share with them. At first some are threatened, some curious, but most respond in very interesting ways. If we don't exchange memories and pass ideas along on, they will be gone, and it will be the children's loss.

Share the games, have fun with young people, then stand back, watch what happens. Children and, yes, teenagers might actually have something to do when they are "hanging out" together. Not only will they have positive ways to entertain themselves, but also they will have common ground, a "safety zone" with adults where laughter, fun and – believe it or not – communication can flow easily.

Handy Ideas

Instead of thinking about all the ways hands can get people into trouble or listing all the axioms about hands, put the fingers and hands into entertaining use.

Hickelty Hackelty Huck

The challenge is to guess the correct number of fingers.

Directions: Two players are required. The first player pats the cadence on the second player's back and chants the rhyme. Player two can't see the number of fingers and makes a guess. Player one responds in the following way, inserting the number guessed and actual fingers held up.

Repeat the rhyme until player two guesses correctly, then the two players switch places.

Hickelty hackelty huck
How many fingers do I hold up?
_____ *you said.*
_____ *it was.*
Hickelty Hackelty Huck

Eency Weency Spider

The challenge is to illustrate the climbing spider while telling the story.

Directions: To form the starting position for Eency Weency Spider, pinch thumb and forefinger together on the right hand and also the left hand, and hold the pinched fingers of both hands together so they look almost like eyeglasses. Twist them forward and back as the spider climbs. Wiggle fingers in a downward motion to simulate rain. Reach over your head so your fingers touch to create the sun. Repeat the climbing spider motion.

Eency weency spider climbs up the water spout
Down comes the rain to wash the spider out.
Out comes the sun and dries up all the rain,
Now eency weency spider climbs up the spout again.

Granny's Cabin

The challenge is to illustrate the story using hands and fingers.

Directions: For the first line, draw an "air outline" of the cabin. Frame your face with both hands to give the appearance of looking out the window in the second line. The bunny ears are formed by raising the second and third fingers while pressing thumb and remaining fingers to the palm of the hand. Have the bunny "hop" by the cabin, then make a fist for the knocking motion. Raise hands in the air for each "Help me." Point forefinger, raise thumb in a gun motion to symbolize the hunter. Use either forefinger or whole hand motion to beckon the bunny into safety.

In her cabin in the wood
Little old granny at the window stood.
She saw a bunny hopping by,
And it tapped upon her door.
"Help me, Help me," the bunny said.
"That old hunter's gonna shoot me dead!"
"Hop inside little bunny dear
"You are safe with me in here."

The rhyme may be repeated over and over, eliminating words and using only gestures until the entire rhyme is motion and swect silence. Begin by speaking and motioning throughout the entire rhyme. Second time use only "air cabin" motion without words but repeat out loud lines two through seven. Third time eliminate the second line except for the window motion. Continue to work through the rhyme until all words are eliminated.

Poor Old Whip-Poor-Wills

The challenge is to create the illusion of disappearing paper.

Directions: Tear two pieces of paper small enough to fit on the fingernail of the forefingers on the right and left hands. Moisten the paper so it will stick on the fingernails. Begin the rhyme with hands behind your back. Reveal the papered forefingers as you say the names. Put the hands behind the back again as the whippoorwills fly away. When they "come back," fold the forefinger into the palm and extend the second finger on each hand. Because the hands move quickly, children don't catch on right away that you have switched fingers.

Poor old whip-poor-wills are sitting on the fence.
One's named Harley and the other's named Spence.
Fly away Harley, fly away Spence.
Come back Harley, come back Spence.

The Church

The challenge is to create a little church with your fingers.

Directions: Lock the fingers of both hands together so that fingers are hidden from sight. Raise the right and left forefingers for the steeple. To open the door spread the thumbs. With palms up and fingers still locked, wiggle the fingers to represent people in my church.

Here is my church
And this is my steeple.
Open my door,
Then greet all the people.

Adam And Eve

The challenge is to trap the other person into saying something undesirable.

Directions: This requires two people. Repeat the riddle and follow through with the listener's command.

Adam and Eve and Pinch Me went out in a boat to fish.
Adam and Eve fell overboard.
Who was left?
(Pinch Me!)

6

Adam and Eve and Tickle Me went down to the lake to swim.
Adam and Eve jumped in.
Who was left on shore?
(Tickle Me!)

Adam and Eve and Hug Me went out to play hide and seek.
Adam and Eve were hiding.
Who was IT?
(Hug Me!)

Jack In The Bush

The challenge is to accurately guess the number of dried corn kernels, beans or rocks held in a closed hand.

Directions: Each player has 20 corn kernels or other small objects in a bag. One player holds an undisclosed number of kernels, rocks etc. in a closed hand. The first player initiates the rhyme, and the second player tries to guess the number of kernels in the first player's hand. If the player guesses correctly, he gets the kernels held in the first player's hand.

Should he guess incorrectly, the second player must give from his supply of kernels the correct amount to the first player. The game is over when one player collects all the kernels; if stopped earlier the winner is the one with the greater number.

Jack in the bush (first player, holding kernels)
Knock him down (second player)
How many licks will it take? (first player)
(Guess a number) (second player)

Rock School

The challenge is to accurately guess in which hand the rock is held.

Directions: Players sit on the top front porch step or interior steps. The "teacher" holds a rock in one hand while keeping both hands concealed behind the back. Teacher asks each student, "In which hand is the rock?" Student selects either right or left.

Teacher reveals the rock. If the student is correct, he/she moves down one step. If incorrect, student remains on same step until he/ she gives correct answer. The first student to the bottom of the stairs becomes the teacher.

Variation: This game may be played on a flat surface such as playground or sidewalk. Draw six chalk lines to represent the steps. Students stay behind lines until "promoted."

Clap Patterns

The challenge is repetition from memory.

Directions: Clap a simple pattern such as one slow, two rapid, one slow. The other person is to repeat the pattern. If the person is successful, he/she may add an additional clap.

This goes back and forth until someone cannot repeat the pattern.

Bingo

The challenge is to replace the BINGO letters with claps.

Directions: Recite this verse spelling out B-I-N-G-O the first time. The first time the verse is repeated replace all B's with a clap. The second repetition of the verse clap in place of "B's" and "I's" then continue the verse repetition so eventually the entire spelling of B-I-N-G-O is replaced with claps.

There was a farmer had a dog
And Bingo was his name-o
B-I-N-G-O, B-I-N-G-O, B-I-N-G-O
And Bingo was his name-o.

Pease Porridge Hot

The challenge is to follow the clap pattern without getting confused as the rhyme speed increases.

Directions: This is the rhyme to use:

Pease porridge hot,
Pease porridge cold,
Pease porridge in the pot
Nine days old.
Some like it hot,
Some like it cold,
Some like it in the pot
Nine days old.

Clapping routine is as follows:

The partners sit opposite each other. Keep in mind each word has its own clap. Three words equal three claps.

On first line: Clap own hands on thighs, clap own hands together, finally clap both hands with partner.

On second line: Repeat the action for first line.

On third line: Clap own hands on thighs, clap own hands together, clap right hands with partner, clap own hands, then clap left hands with partner.

On fourth line: Repeat the action for the first line.

The clap pattern is repeated for the remaining four lines. After each eight lines is completed, say the rhyme a little faster until words go too quickly for the clap activity, and one partner gets confused breaking the routine.

Clapping routine variation:

On first line: Clap own hands on thighs, clap own hands together, and clap right hands with partner.

On second line: Repeat first two motions for the first two words in line one but this time on the third word clap left hands with partner.

On third line: Repeat first two motions; clap right hands with partner, then clap own hands together.

On fourth line: Clap left hands with partner, clap own hands together, then clap both hands with partner.

The clap pattern is repeated for the remaining four lines.

Pile On

The challenge is to see how fast you can pile on hands without getting any hands out of order.

Directions: The first player puts the right hand, palm down, on a flat surface. The second player puts right hand on top of the first hand. Next, first player puts left hand on top of second player's right hand, then second player puts his left hand on top of the pile.

First player slowly pulls right hand from the bottom of the pile and places it on top. The second player's hand becomes the bottom hand, so he/she pulls it from the bottom of the pile and places it on top.

Continue pulling out hands from the bottom of the pile and putting them on top, going faster and faster until one of the players moves a hand out of order.

Smack

(Also Called Electric Shock Or Palms Up)

The challenge is to quickly reposition hands in order to smack the opponent's hands.

Directions: Two players stand facing each other. One player holds out both hands with the palms up, and the other player places hands palms down on the opponent's upturned hands.

It is the task of the lower hands to move up, turn over and smack the backs of one or both hands before the opponent can move them. They continue in this position as long as the bottom hands can slap one or both of the top hands. When the bottom hands fail to make contact, then the positions are reversed, top moves to palms up and bottom must move palms down to the top.

The players alternate the top and bottom positions for as long as they want to continue the game.

Counting Out
Ways To Choose Sides, Settle Disputes and Determine Who is "it."

Counting Potatoes
The challenge is to be the last person counted out.

Directions: Participants stand in a circle, holding out both hands clenched in fists. The counter, also with clenched fists, starts by tapping own fist to begin the count. When the counter touches "More," that hand goes behind the player's back and the counting continues until one fist is left in the circle. The counter remains in the circle and continues counting even when counted out.

One potato, two potatoes,
Three potatoes, four,
Five potatoes, six potatoes
Seven potatoes, more.

Monkey Business
The challenge is to be the one selected to be leader, captain or "it." Directions: Participants stand or sit in a circle. Someone walks around behind and taps each person on the shoulder while reciting the rhyme. Players are not eliminated, but the person tapped at the conclusion of the rhyme is selected.

Eenie, meenie, minie, moe,
Catch that monkey by his toe;
And if he hollers let him go,
Eenie, meenie, minie, moe!

Eenie, meeny, miney, moe,
Catch a monkey by the toe;
And if he hollers make him pay
Fifty dollars every day!

Monkey, monkey in the tree,
How many monkeys do we see?
One, two, three, etc. (the last number counted is "it.")

Monkey, monkey built a car
How many wheels do you think there are?
One, two, three, four! (the person tapped on four is "it.")

O-U-T

The challenge is to determine the leader by being the first one "out."

Directions: The same circle and tapping as Monkey Business

Wire, brier, slippery rock!
Three old seagulls in a flock!
One flew east, one flew west,
One flew over the osprey's nest.
O-U-T spells out,
And out you go.

William Trimbletoe
He's a good fisherman
Catches hens, puts 'em in pens
Some lay eggs and some do not
Wire, brier, limber-lock
Three geese in a flock
One flew east, one flew west
One flew over the chickadee's nest
Be-you-gone-out-home
You-dirty-dish-rag-YOU!
(The one tapped on YOU is out – or "it.")

Apples, cherries, peaches and plums.
Tell me when your birthday comes.
(The person tapped on "comes" says month and date of birth.)
Resume tapping while counting out the date: December 16 (count

from 1 to 16), May 24 (count from 1 to 24).
   And you are O-U-T.

More Hand Games

Pick A Hand
(Sometimes known as Holder)
   The challenge is avoid the hand that holds the object. The one who finds the object is "it."

   Directions: The person with the object (a small pebble, coin or button) holds both hands behind his/her back to shift the object from hand to hand between guessing rounds. When ready, the holder extends both fists for the guesser to tap one fist. The holder opens the tapped fist to reveal either the object or an empty hand. If the object is there, the guesser loses and is "it."

Button Button
   The challenge is for one player to locate a button, coin or rock concealed in a hand.

   Directions: One person stands in the center of a circle and says, "Button, button, who's got the button?"

   As the "button" is passed from one player to another, the hands of all players are in motion as if giving or receiving the button. The person in the center has one guess. If the guess is correct, the guesser and the holder change places. With an incorrect guess the center player again repeats. "Button, button, who's got the button?" to activate the passing. The guessing begins again.

Heads or Tails
   The challenge is to call the correct side of the coin.

   Directions: As one person flips or tosses the coin in the air the other calls out either "Heads" or "Tails." If the call is "Heads" and the coin lands "Heads up", the caller is the winner. The coin must land flat. If it is on a slant, the flip must be done over.

   The coin may also be tossed caught in the closed right hand, and revealed on the back of the left hand. Sometimes the toss is extended to best three out of five. If a major decision or controversy is being settled between two people, the winning side should be determined before the flip. The calls are made while the coin is in the air.

Scissors, Paper and Stone

The challenge is to flash the powerful hand symbol which will overcome the other symbols. This helps pass the time, however captainship or "it" may be decided by the most powerful symbol. or who lasts in the circle the longest.

Directions: Determine the symbols.

Stone (fist)

Scissors (fist with second and third fingers extended like scissor blades)

Paper (open hand)

Determine the power:

Stone makes scissors dull.

Scissors cut paper

Paper wraps stone

Play: Two players stand opposite, each with one hand behind the back. Someone counts 1-2-3. On three, both flash a symbol. Survey the symbols to determine who is overpowered. The combination varies with each flash.

Flash, or Odds or Evens

The challenge is to reveal an odd or even number of fingers to correspond with the call when the caller says "odds" or "evens."

Directions: Participants sit or stand across from each other (or in a circle for a group) with their hands behind their backs. Someone counts 1-2-3. On the count of three, as the players simultaneously show specific fingers (ex. 3 on one hand, 4 on the other) the caller says odd or even. If the call is even and the player has flashed (count the fingers on both hands) an even number, he/she stays in. Flashing odd when even is called or vice versa means elimination. To keep score award a point to each for the correct flash. The game is over when someone has accumulated five points.

Jacks

The challenge is picking up a designated number of jacks without letting the ball bounce. There are as many variations in the game of Jacks as there are children playing it.

Directions For Basic Jacks: Sometimes a circle is outlined by drawing with chalk or marking with string, but clearly defined boundaries are not necessary. Toss 5 jacks in the circle. Call "one-zees" and toss the ball in the air. While the ball is in the air grab one jack. Catch it with the hand used to collect jacks. Repeat "one-zees" until all the jacks are collected or until the ball bounces. Then it is another person-'s turn. If it is a solo game, then the player may advance, Round two is "two-zees," and two jacks are collected in the same "beat the bounce" manner until the count reaches the point where all the jacks must be collected in one sweep. If at anytime a player makes a mistake, the count automatically returns to "one-zees."

Elevens

The challenge is coordinating hand-to-hand exchange with one bounce of the ball.

Toss the jacks on the ground and throw the ball in the air. Pick up a jack with one hand, transfer it to the other hand, and let the ball bounce once before catching it in the empty hand. That is one point. Pick up one jack at a time in this manner until a score of 11 is reached.

Twenty-Fives

The challenge is coordinating hand to hand exchange before the ball bounces twice.

Spread the jacks, and toss the ball in the air. Pick up five jacks in one hand, shift the jacks to the other hand before the ball can bounce a second time. Catch the ball in the empty hand. The game ends when the point tally reaches 25.

Knock-Knock

The challenge is knocking to beat the bounce.

Spread the jacks, and toss the ball in the air. Pick up one jack, knock once on the floor with your knuckles and catch the ball before it bounces. Advanced players try to knock once for one-zees, twice for two-zees etc.

Rock-A-Bye

The challenge is to rock the baby before the second bounce of the ball.

Spread the jacks and toss the ball in the air. Collect one jack, cross your arms over your chest and pretend to rock the baby back and forth before catching the ball after the first bounce. Work up to "five-zees."

Marbles

There is quite a large vocabulary that goes with the game of marbles. Some commonly used terms are as follows:

Circling – Moving about to determine the best spot outside the ring to take the shot.

Edgers – Marbles that roll near the edge of the ring, staying within the ring.

For Fair – The marbles won by the opponent are returned to the original owner at the end of the game.

For Keeps – The marbles won by the opponent are kept at the end of the game.

Hunching – An illegal crossing of the hand over the ring line as the shot is taken.

Knuckling Down – This refers to the position of the hand when taking a shot. One knuckle must touch the ground and remain in that position until the taw (shooter) leaves the player's hand. The marble is cradled in the forefinger and shot out by a flick of the thumb.

Lag line – A long horizontal line drawn along one side of the ring and touching it at some point is used to determine shooting order. Players stand or kneel at the pitch line and toss their taws towards the lag line. Whoever comes closest to the line without crossing it gets to go first.

Miss – The player takes a shot and fails to knock a marble out of the ring.

Pitch line – A long horizontal line that runs parallel on the opposite side of the circle to the lag line. To "lag" each player stands or kneels behind this line, knuckles down or tosses his taw towards the lag line.

Taw – A marble 1/2" to 3/4" in diameter used as the "shooter."

Holding Steady

The challenge is to knock the opponent's marbles outside the ring.

Directions: Cluster twelve or more marbles in the center of a circle 8 feet in diameter. After shooting order is determined, find a spot to knuckle down then shoot. Each marble that is struck and goes outside the ring is one point. The player who makes the hit, driving a marble out of the ring, gets to shoot again.

If the taw knocks a marble out, but stays within the ring, the player may assume the knuckle down position where the taw rests. If at any time a player fails to knock the marble out of the ring, he reclaims his taw and the turn passes to the next player.

Hunching Boston

The challenge is to shoot with great force in any position to knock marbles out of the ring.

Directions: The same rules as for Holding Steady apply except for the method of shooting. The player has unlimited movement of hand while shooting.

Cincy

The challenge is to knock marbles out of the ring without having the taw hit.

Directions: The circle is 4 feet in diameter, with a line drawn through the center. After marbles are evenly spaced along the center line of the circle, the players stand a distance of 10 to 15 feet away from the circle. They toss their taws at the center line of the circle. The taw landing closest but not passing the center line goes first. The other players shoot in order according to the proximity of their taws to the center line.

The first shot is knuckle down outside the ring but following shots are taken wherever the taw lands. In the event that one player's taw hits another player's taw, the player who is hit is out of the game, and all the marbles won by the ejected player are returned to the circle.

All marbles held by each player at the end of the game equal one point each.

Chaser, Stalker, Or Murder

The challenge is to be the last player to stay in the game.

Directions: After the size of the circle and the shooting order are determined, cluster the marbles in the center of the circle. The first player shoots until there is a miss, and then the second player shoots etc. Should one player hit another the taw of another player, the hit player is out of the game, but the other player continues to shoot until a miss occurs.

Players try to shoot marbles out of the ring, hit marbles of others and stay out of the way so as not to be hit and thus "killed."

Picking Plums

The challenge is to pick as many "plums" (win as many marbles) as possible.

Directions: Draw two parallel lines approximately 6 feet apart. After shooting order is determined, each player must place three marbles 3 inches apart on the far line, then use the near line to knuckle down. Each player gets one shot per round, and any marbles knocked off the line during that turn may be collected by the shooter.

If a player doesn't hit a "plum," he must add a marble to the row of marbles on the line. When the all the "plums" have been picked off the line the game is over, and the players get one point for each "plum."

Bean Bags

Although tossed, juggled, or passed like a ball, bean bags are an entity unto themselves. Perhaps the inventor of the bean bag chair drew inspiration by carrying around a little hand sewn, hand size, scrunchy bean bag. Any old scrap of heavy fabric will do. However the composition of the filling is up for discussion.

I found early on that a little bag filled with beans stings, if someone hurls it with intent to hurt. Occasionally, even a double-stitched bean bag seam will split with the weight of dried beans. Invariably, a three or four year old will see loose beans and follow that horrendous unwritten code of childhood, "See if a bean will fit in my nose!"

Although a nuisance to clean up, rice or wild bird seed are inexpensive alternative fillings.

Jiffy Bean Bags And Toss Targets

MATERIALS:

Two 5" X 5" squares of heavy fabric such as denim or felt in any color or design

Fabric glue

Bird seed or rice for filling

Scoop or serving spoon

Plastic containers in three sizes (large soft drink bottles, 1.2-gallon and 1-gallon milk jugs etc.)

Sharp knife or scissors

Felt tip marking pen

Colorful plastic tape

Directions: With right sides of the fabric together, stitch twice around three sides and all but two inches of the fourth side. Trim the corners close to the stitching. Turn the bag right side out and using the scoop or spoon, fill the bag with approximately one cup of filling. The contents of the bag should be loose and "scrunchy," not tightly packed.

Turn the raw edges in and glue the bag closed.

Bean bags may be personalized by writing, drawing, etc. with the felt tip pens or cutting and gluing initials from felt or other fabric.

Hint: When using felt, cut squares with pinking shears and instead of having to turn, stitch on the outside. Felt is easy to work with, so bean bags can be made in various shapes.

Directions For Making Jug Targets: Cut the tops from three plastic jugs so that they are all approximately 7 inches high. Run plastic tape around the cut edge of the container, folding it over to make a smooth, finished edge. With a felt tip marking pen, write a point value such as 1, 5 or 10 on each jug. Assign the smallest jug the highest point value.

For younger children use one large jug or place a weight in the bottom of each jug to avoid that frustration which comes with "tipping." Designate a real or imagined "toe line" to stand behind.

Variation: Make a box target from a sturdy cardboard box. With the felt tip marking pen draw one large circle in the center of one side of the box. Surround the large circle with four smaller circles. Cut out the circles and under each opening write an assigned point value. Children may wish to paint the target box or glue fabric or magazine pictures in a decorative collage.

Having A Ball

The ball of choice is pale pink and somewhat spongy although a firm rubber ball or tennis ball will do. The space age composition balls that bounce extra high or in an erratic manner are a frustration rather than an asset to traditional ball games where skill-bouncing is an art.

John's Long Island Stoop Hit And Fly Ball

The challenge is to bounce the ball off the front stoop (step) so the person behind you can't catch it.

Directions: Two or more people can play. Everyone faces the front step. The pitcher stands 3 feet from the step while the others position themselves behind the pitcher. The pitcher angles the ball at the step so it bounces off the step and flies behind him. The player behind the pitcher tries to catch the "fly" ball. If successful, that player becomes the pitcher, but if he fails then it is a hit, and the pitcher continues until a fly is caught.

Hint: Angle the ball at the edge of the step for a high fly ball or direct the ball to the angle formed where the steps meet for a fast "grounder".

Call Ball

The challenge is to catch the ball without letting it bounce when your name is called.

Directions: Players stand facing a wall, and one player throws the ball at the wall calling out the name of another player. The player whose name is called must catch the ball directly from the wall without letting it bounce on the ground. If the player successfully catches the ball, he/she tosses it off the wall calling another player's name. If the player does not catch the ball, the turn goes back to the last caller.

A! My Name Is Annie

The challenge is to bounce the letters all the way through the alphabet, catching the ball each time on the first bounce.

Directions: Holding a tennis or rubber ball in the right hand, bounce it, step over it with the left leg, and catch the ball in the left hand. As the ball bounces say, "A! My name is Annie!" then on the next bounce say "B! My name is Betsy!" Continue, "C! My name is Connie!" and so on until every letter has been called or the ball is missed.

Hint: If more than one ball is available, this is a good side-by-side game to play with a friend.

Variation 1: Throw the ball against a wall and catch without dropping it while repeating the rhyme.

Variation 2: Call boys names rather than girls.

Seven Up

The challenge is to toss the ball up in the air, clap hands a designated number of times, and catch the ball before the second bounce.

Directions: The player tosses a tennis or rubber ball in the air calling "one up!" As the ball bounces once, the player claps hands one time then catches the ball.

The player tosses the ball in the air calling "two up!", claps twice and catches it after the first bounce. This continues until the count reaches "seven up!" After seven then the order reverses going six, five, etc. with the corresponding number of claps. The game is over when the player goes through the counting clapping cycle or drops the ball.

Hint: Not only is this is a good solo game but also for side by side play with a friend.

Annie Over

The challenge is to throw the ball over the house or garage roof and catch those waiting to receive on the other side.

Directions: One person or one group stands in front while a second person or group stands behind the house or garage. A person in front yard holds the ball and yells, "Annie," and a person in back answers "over."

The ball is thrown over the roof. At the time the ball is thrown over the house or garage, players reverse positions. The people in front run around to the back and try to catch the person who caught the ball. Simultaneously, the person in the back who catches the ball tries to run around to the front yard without getting caught. When it reaches the point that everyone is on one side leaving no one to receive, the game is finished.

Hint: Sometimes the people in front or back send spies to see which route around the house the opposition will take. If the spy gets caught "spying" he/she is captured by the opposition.

Florence's Roly Poly

The challenge is to roll the ball, hop to the square, and bounce the ball without touching or going outside the boundary lines.

Directions: Mark off a rectangle in the dirt or on the sidewalk approximately two feet across and three feet up. Mark off six equal squares two by two, side by side. To number the squares, begin at the bottom start line and work in a column up the left side to the top 1,2,3.

At the top begin the new column with 4, working down the right side 5 then 6 to the start line. Just behind the start line is "home."

Roll the ball to square 1, hop on one foot to square 1, pick up the ball, bounce it once, then hop back to "home." From "home" roll the ball to square 2, hop to that square and bounce the ball the appropriate number of times. Continue rolling, hopping and bouncing through the six squares. There are no short cuts! Even though square 6 is adjacent to home, the player must hop the entire 1 to 5 circuit before reaching 6.

The game is over when the player completes the circuit or steps on the line or "out of bounds." Alternate turns if more than one is playing.

Hopscotch

The challenge is to hop through the diagram without losing balance or stepping on boundary lines.

Directions: Select a rock to use as a marker. The player stands behind the designated toss line which is back from the starting line and tosses the marker, aiming for the block marked 1. If successful, the player hops on one foot into the space marked 1, still on one foot bends over and picks up the marker, stands up and hops back to home.

Now the player aims the marker at the space 2. The player must hop on space 1 to get to 2, use the one foot retrieval system and hop home.

When the player reaches side by side squares, he/she may put one foot in each square, providing the marker is not in one of them.

The activity continues until the player

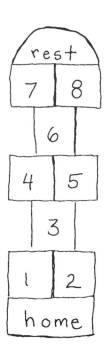

makes a mistake such as putting a hand or other foot on the ground, failing to pick up the stone, or tossing the stone in the wrong square or on a boundary line.

Hint: Some players prefer to reach behind and hold one foot up while hopping. (Left hand holds left foot or right holds right.)

Jumping Rope and Other Games

It is interesting to see the growing popularity in rope jumping as a physical fitness activity. Note the plethora of video tapes which teach adults how to jump and skip rope for fitness. As fashion dictates, some sporting goods stores have designated departments for state of the art jumping ropes, special shoes, sweat bands and ropes with swivel handles.

Really, all it takes is a little space and a length of rope. My daughter and her friends kept lengths of clothes line which were adjustable. They wrapped it around their hands to make it just the right length for solo jumping or when necessary unrolled it to accommodate two turners and a jumper. Sometimes they "Double Dutched" using the fancy rocker step instead of the traditional jump, turning two ropes at once. Sometimes two jumpers went at a time. They did "Red Hot Peppers" turning the rope extra fast when the rhyme was complete and the counting began.

When a third person wasn't available and two people wanted to play jump rope, they tied one end of the rope around a skinny tree. One turned the free end of the rope while the other jumped.

Whenever I ask anyone about jumping rope chants, I get a momentary blank look, then the smile, hear maybe a line at first. Then out tumbles a fragment, then the entire rhyme. There are so many rhymes, so many variations.

The rhymes collected here are ones passed around in my family and collected from friends. Perhaps you will recognize old friends, meet new ones, but what is important is to preserve jumping cadences and pass them along. Why don't you dig up a rope, go outside and jump to a few of them? It could be more fun than a video! The price is right, too!

To begin any jumping rhyme, the jumper runs into the turning rope, gets three warmup jumps and calls out the name of the selected chant. The player jumps through the chant and exits the turning rope at the successful conclusion of the jump. For a variation, after the three warmup jumps, one of the turners may call out the name of the chant. The jumper must jump to the "Turner's Choice.".

Jumping Rhymes
CINDERELLA
Cinderella dressed in yellow
Went upstairs to kiss a fella.
Her mistake, she kissed a snake
How many doctors did it take?
1-2-3-4 etc. (Optional: RED HOT PEPPERS!)

MARY
Mary lost her ribbon,
Mary lost her hat,
Mary lost her fifty cents.
What do you think of that?

Mary found her ribbon
Mary found her hat,
Mary found her fifty cents,
What do you think of that?

TEDDY BEAR

(Jumpers are to follow the directions in the rhymes.)
Teddy bear, teddy bear, turn around,
Teddy bear, teddy bear, touch the ground.
Teddy bear, teddy bear, tap your toe,
Teddy bear, teddy bear, out you go!

Teddy bear, teddy bear, go upstairs.
Teddy bear, teddy bear, say your prayers.
Teddy bear, teddy bear, shut the light,
Teddy bear, teddy bear, say good-night.

BABY CARRIAGE

(Boy's name) and (girl's name) sitting in a tree
K-I-S-S-I-N-G
First comes love, then comes marriage,
Then comes (name) with a baby carriage.
(RED HOT PEPPERS follows until the jumper misses.)

RIN TIN TIN

Rin Tin Tin, swallowed a pin,
Went to the doctor and the doctor wasn't in.
He opened the door and fell on the floor,
And that was the end and there is no more...
EXCEPT RED HOT PEPPERS! (jump until turners give out or jumper misses.)

THE GOLDEN RULE

Brother and sister went to school,
Tried to learn the Golden Rule.
How many lessons did it take?
1-2-3-4-5-6 (until the jumper misses)

POLICEMAN

Policeman, policeman, do your duty,
Here comes (girl's name), the American beauty.
She can wiggle, she can waggle,
She can do the split,
But I bet you any money she can't do this.
(Jumper does a stunt or trick and jumps out of the turning rope.)

SET THE TABLE
Mabel, Mabel, set the table.
Don't forget the salt, mustard, vinegar
and RED HOT PEPPERS (Rope turners increase turning speed until jumper misses)

STRAWBERRY SHORTCAKE
Strawberry shortcake, raspberry tart,
Tell me the name of my sweetheart.
A-B-C-D-E...(As the rope turners say the alphabet, they speed up the rope until the jumper misses. The letter that sends the jumper out is the initial of her sweetheart's name.)

THE WEATHER
Here we are together,
When do you like the weather?
*In January, February, March...(*With each month the rope turners speed up the rope until the jumper misses.)

CHARLIE OVER THE WATER
Charlie over the water,
Charlie over the sea,
Charlie saw some blackbirds,
Sitting in a tree.
How many blackbirds did he see?
1-2-3-4-5 (Count goes on until the jumper misses.)

HOUSE FOR RENT
This is not an elimination-by-miss jump. The jumper says the rhyme and designates the next jumper.
House for rent,
Inquire within;
When I move out
Let (Name) move in.

HORSIE'S IN THE MEADOW
Horsie's in the meadow
Cow's in the corn
Now you've got to name the month
That you were born.
January, February, March

(Jump out on your birthday month)

ORDER IN THE COURT
Order in the court
The judge is eating greens.
His wife climbed in the bathtub
To sink some submarines.
How many did she sink?
1-2-3-4-5-6-7-8
(Jump to the count until a miss)

LITTLE MISS
Miss, miss, little miss:
When she misses, she misses like this.
(The jumper intentionally steps on the rope to stop it.)

I HAD A LITTLE SISTER
I had a little sister
Her name was baby Sue.
I put her in the bathtub
To see what she would do.
She drank most all the water
She ate a chunk of soap
And laid out on the bathroom floor
Got a bubble in her throat.
I called for the doctor
Who called for his nurse
Who called for the lady
With the alligator purse.
Burp said the doctor
Burp said his nurse
Burp said the lady
With the alligator purse.
Bye said the doctor
Bye said his nurse
Bye said the lady
With the alligator purse.
Out goes the doctor
Out goes his nurse
Out goes the lady
With the alligator purse.

(If the jumper has lasted the duration of the rhyme, on the last "Out goes" the jumper jumps out.)

DOWN IN THE MEADOW
Down in the meadow
Where the green grass grows
There sat (jumper)
As sweet as a rose.
She sang, she sang,
She sang so sweet
Till along come a fella
And kissed her on the cheek
How many kisses did she receive?
(Ah-1, ah-2, ah-3, etc.)

High Water/Low Water
The challenge is according to the height of the rope: jump over or crawl under without touching the rope.

Directions: The rope holders have the rope slack on the ground as the player steps over it. With each step over, the holders raise the rope a few inches. Finally, there comes a point when the player no longer can step or jump over the rope without touching it. This is a signal to the holders to begin to lower the rope a few inches at a time as the player goes under the rope. This continues until the player can no longer go under the rope with out touching it. When this happens, another player has a turn.

Beneath The Arch
The challenge is to run under the rope as it is in the upward swing without touching it.

Directions: The holders turn the rope and each player takes a turn running "under the arch." Touching the rope is an automatic out of the game. The winner is the remaining person in the game.

Wiggle-Worm
(Sometimes called Sidewinder or Rattlesnake)
The challenge is to hop over the wiggling rope without touching it.

Directions: The holders wiggle the rope from side to side while the jumper tries to hop over the "Wiggle-Worm" rope without touching it. After all others have been eliminated by touching the rope, the winner is the one who has not touched the rope.

Jump The Creek

The challenge is to jump over the rope designated creek without getting your feet wet.

Directions: Rope holders place two jump ropes side by side in straight lines on the ground. The ropes represent the banks of the creek. Using both feet, player tries to jump the creek. After each jump, the holders move the ropes further apart until the creek is so wide that the player steps in and gets his/her feet wet.

Variation: Try to jump the creek by hopping on one foot.

Other Action Games
Hide And Go Seek

Although there are many elaborate variations, this is a basic form. The challenge is to get "home free" without being seen by "it."

Directions: Use Potatoes or a personal favorite method of counting out to determine which player is "it." The person who is "it" stands at a designated location, "home" (a tree, porch step, porch railing etc.) and loudly counts to 100.

During the counting the other players run and hide. When the count reaches 100, "it" calls out "Ready or not, here I come!" and searches for the players. When "it" spots a player he/she calls out the name of the player and runs for "home" and taps home three times saying, "1-2-3 on (name)."

If the player outruns "it" and reaches "home" before "it," the player says, "1-2-3 home free." The game is over when all players have come back to "home." The first person (or last) caught becomes "it," and the game begins again. If the game has to stop or "it" simply gives up and can't find the hiders, "it" calls "Allee, allee in free," and the players emerge from their hiding places.

Variation: The rules are the same except before the hunt, "it" calls out the following rhyme:

Bushel of wheat,
Bushel of rye,
All not hid,
Holler "I."

If someone does "holler I," then "it" counts to 100 by tens and calls out:

Bushel of wheat
Bushel of clover,
All not hid,
Can't hide over.
All eyes open, here I come!

Kick The Can

The challenge is to find the hidden players before one of them kicks the can.

Directions: An empty tin can is placed in the middle of a large (10'-15' diameter) circle. The person who has been designated as "it" covers his/her eyes and counts to 20 using the Mississippi method while the others hide. (This counting method goes as follows: 1 Mississippi, 2 Mississippi, 3 Mississippi finally to 20 Mississippi.)

As "it" captures the hiders, he/she puts them in jail, which is within the big circle. While "it" continues to look for hidden players, any player still hiding can run into the circle and kick the can outside the ring, free the prisoners, and all may hide again.

If the hider who is trying to kick the can is spotted by "it," and "it" can tag him/her before the can goes outside the circle, the tagged player is captured and becomes a prisoner in jail.

The game continues this way until all players outside the circle are tagged and taken prisoner.

Hint: Should "it" become discouraged or should the game have to end before all are tagged and taken prisoner, "it" shouts, "Allee, allee, in free" to signal all players that the game is over.

Wood Tag

The challenge is to touch wood to avoid being tagged.

Directions: This is a tag game where a designated "it" must catch other players. A player about to be tagged can touch a piece of wood such as a tree, porch railing, fence post etc. and be "safe." The player may be saved by touching wood three times but may not touch and be saved by the same wood more than once. As "it" tags someone he/she says, "Tag! You're it!" There is a new "it," and the game begins again.

Squat Tag

The challenge is to squat low to the ground before being tagged.

Directions: This is a tag game where a designated "it" must tap another player before the player is able to get into a squat position. To squat allows one to be safe from tagging. To be safe the player can't just bend over; he/she must have legs bent, crouched low to the ground. The first person tagged becomes "it," and the game begins again.

Sunshine And Shadow Tag

The challenge is to step on the other player's shadow.

Directions: This is a game for two players. One is designated as "it" and the other is the runner. "it" gives the runner a count of 1-2-3 for a head start. "it" tries to step on the other player's shadow. When that happens the roles reverse, the runner becomes "it," and the game begins again.

To avoid being tagged, the runner may step into a shaded area (safety zone) twice so that the shadow disappears. If the player stays in the shaded area longer than the count of 1-2-3-, he/she becomes "it."

Freeze Tag

The challenge is to touch "home" base before being tagged and frozen by "it."

Directions: The designated "it" counts to five, giving the players a running start. "it" chases the players and as they are tagged, they must freeze in that position, no matter how ridiculous that position may be until all players are "frozen" or someone reaches "home."

The player to touch home is the new "it." If all players are tagged, the one frozen in the most unusual position, as determined by the old "it", becomes the new "it."

Variation: The players freeze in order to avoid being tagged by "it."

Swinger's Statue

The challenge is after being swung by the "swinger," to maintain that position without moving.

Directions: The designated "swinger" takes a player by the hand, pivots and brings the player full circle before releasing. The player must become a statue and remain in that position until all other players are swung and released. The swinger selects the most unusual pose. That statue becomes the swinger.

Red Light, Green Light
(Sometimes called Creeping Statue or Statue Race)

The challenge is to be the first player to reach the finish line without being seen in motion by "it."

Directions: Establish a start line about 20 feet from the finish line. All players stand behind the start line, while "it" stands with back to players about 5 feet beyond the finish line.

With back turned to the players, "it" shouts "Green Light." All players try to move swiftly and quietly to the finish line. At any time "it" may call out, "Red Light" and quickly turn around. Players must stop instantly where they are and remain motionless, holding the position. If "it" sees a player move, that player must go back to the start line.

"It" continues to turn back to players and shouts, "Green Light" then "Red Light" until a player reaches the finish line. The first to reach the finish line becomes the new "it," and the game begins again.

Follow The Leader

The challenge is to mimic every action of the leader.

Directions: Players line up behind the leader. They are led around the yard or through the house and mimic the activities of the leader as they chant:

We're following the leader,
The leader, the leader
We're following the leader
To see what (he/she) can do.

At the conclusion of the chant, the leader performs an action such as hopping and patting the head, walking three times around a tree or chair, twirling-around walking, skipping backwards etc.

If everyone is successful mimicking the leader, the leader moves to the back of the line and the next person becomes leader. If any follower makes a mistake that person moves to the back of the line, and the same leader continues to try to trick the players.

Hint: This is a wonderful adult/child combination game. Children are very creative and flexible in the ways they move and often can fool adults...and we all know what fun that can be.

Variation: In some regions Follow The Leader is called Monkey See. The following premise is the same but this time the leader chants:

Monkey see, monkey do
Can you do what I can do?

Simon Says
(Sometimes called Captain Sez)

The challenge is to mimic the activity of the leader when the correct command is given.

Directions: Since this is a game of physical feats, have players space themselves so they have room to "get active." The leader calls out and performs a command such as, "Simon says, "Touch your toes." The players follow the command. If the command is not preceded with "Simon Says," the players are to remain motionless. A player who fails to follow a "Simon Says" command immediately or obeys a command not prefaced by "Simon Says" must drop out of the game. The last one in the game gets to be the next Simon.

Remember, each time a command is given with or without "Simon says," the leader performs the activity in an effort to confuse the followers.

Mother May I?

The challenge is to be the first one to reach Mother (the finish line).

Directions: "MOTHER" (the leader) stands at the finish line. The players stand a distance (10'-15') from "MOTHER" and request permission to take a certain number of steps forward. "MOTHER" either grants or denies the request by changing it to something that suits her.

Players may try to sneak behind "MOTHER'S" back, inching up toward the finish line. If sneaking is detected, "MOTHER" sends the offender back to the start line.

The winner, the first to cross the finish line, becomes "MOTHER."

A typical request could be, "MOTHER may I please take three giant steps forward?" Because "MOTHER" controls the activity, "MOTHER" could respond, "Yes you may take three giant steps forward," She could reply, "No, you may take one giant step forward," or "No, you may take two baby steps forward," or "No, you may take two giant steps backwards."

Some "MOTHER" approved steps: Giant step (exaggerated step moving forward as far as possible)

Giant hop or skip (exaggerated etc.)

Baby step (smallest possible step)

Regular Hop or Skip step (one foot)

Regular Jumping step (both feet)

Umbrella step (done by putting a finger on the crown of the head and twirling once.)

Elephant step (done by bending at the waist, clasping hands and swinging them like an elephant's trunk)

Frog step (done in squat position, leaping like a frog)

Russian step (done by squatting down, folding arms across chest and taking a step while in this squatting position)

Chicken step (done by bending down, putting arms between legs, grabbing hold of the outside of the ankles, and stepping one foot then the other)

The Backyard Naturalist

The major requirements to become a backyard naturalist are time and patience. Apartment dwellers, take heart! Contrary to thought backyard isn't necessarily limited to the area around your place of residence. Backyard can be a state of mind. Find an open space where you can spread your arms and not touch anything on either side. Take advantage of parks and green spaces. Begin in a general way during any season in any location at any time of day or night. Plan later to set aside a time for thorough investigation. You will find specific suggestions in this section after you have learned to simplify.

The Backyard Experience

Stand on a back step, a balcony, a spot just outside your door. Close your eyes, inhale, then exhale. With your eyes still closed take another deep breath stretching your arms above your head as you inhale. Lower your arms as you exhale. Is the air hot and humid? Is it cold to your nose, throat, and lungs? Is the air fragrant with flowers, heavy with wood smoke, acrid from automobile exhaust or an oil refinery? Savor the air.

The season is unimportant. Choose a time of day, morning, noon, or evening. "Experience the air" six days consecutively. No matter how small, make note of any differences in the air. Is there something you anticipate happening, perhaps the warmth of the sun on your face? What is your inclination if it rains? Do you say forget it? NO! Get out there and turn your face up to the rain. What happens on the seventh day? Do you miss your backyard breath of air?

The Sounds Of Backyard Life

In a survey conducted in the Tidewater region of Virginia, employers were asked to rate the most desirable qualities in workers hired directly after high school graduation. The survey showed on a scale of one to eight, listening skills ranked second with honesty as number one. More than ever it is important to unplug and re-sensitize, cultivate the forgotten art of listening.

Consider from *Walden,* Henry David Thoreau's thoughts on listening: "The morning wind forever blows, the poem of creation is uninterrupted; but few are the ears that hear it." Take life's pulse. Stand on the back step with closed eyes and listen to the yard sounds. The first sounds of morning are far different from the backyard settling in for the night sounds. I know when the winds shift to the northeast because the limbs on our big old oak tree groan. The pine branches tap together when the wind reaches 15 mph from the south. At ten after seven most mornings my neighbor needs three attempts before her car starts. The mockingbird changes her tune when the bushy gray cat passes through the yard, and the squirrels sound like crying babies when they get irritated with my dog, Josie.

These big sounds reassure me that all is well so far in this day. Don't be satisfied with the obvious noises. Listen for the small sounds, your breath sounds.

The Backyard Walk

This is not suggesting a cardiovascular speed walk; rather, a quiet observation tour of the yard. A city park is an option for apartment dwellers. Teachers might free the children and walk around the school yard. If you have one, take that handy companion, the magnifying glass. Begin with short jaunts; put away for the moment grandiose thoughts of full-fledged interpretive nature walks at state parks with a tour guide, back pack and picnic. What you observe depends upon the time of year so get to know your yard season by season. Consider the lesson learned by Voltaire's Candide, who searched the world over for happiness and found the secret to true happiness was in cultivating his own garden. Cultivate your garden, walk your own property.

Sometimes, children enjoy thematic walks. They derive a certain security from knowing the overall plan. A thematic walk does free a structured, programmed child from the anxiety of the unknown. The child is susceptible to spontaneity! To get underway you might consider some of my favorite walks: Signs Of Spring Walk, Midsummer Night's Walk, Hint Of Autumn Walk, or Bundle Up Winter Is Here Walk. Why not try a Penny Walk or a Too Tired To Walk Walk?

It is not my plan to tell you how, where or when to walk, but rather to interest you in "doing your own thing." Give yourself an Emersonian posture as you consider an idea from his essay, *Self-Reliance*, that "Whoso would be a man must be a non-conformist." The walks discussed here have been pleasurable over the years for my children, my dogs, and me. The hints, observations, discussions and explanations come from many walks as a parent, a teacher and romantic person. If you accept observations from my journal entries, family reminiscences and experience as motivation, consider Emily Dickinson's closing thoughts about Nature from her poem, "This Is My Letter To The World:"

For love of her, sweet countryman,
Judge tenderly of me!

Signs Of Spring Walk

Walk when all is seemingly bleak with no hint of green. You might assume that little made it through the winter freeze. Take a stick and carefully, gently turn over a mound of damp leaves located in a protected area, against a house, fence or shed. Have your magnifying glass handy. It might take two or three probes, but your reward for perseverance will be a peek at living things in motion. Many times you will find centipedes, bugs, beetles and possibly spiders. Other leaf mounds may yield white to pale green shoots of hardy plants. Curled-up fern shoots look like little white question marks.

Whether you are on coastal flatland or in the mountains you will be able to find the early spring violet. Near the coast the early violets have long stems and good-size leaves. Violets adapt to their surroundings. One late April day, I was on my mountain in Pocahontas County, West Virginia, hoping for signs of spring but resigned to the fact that the ground had yet to thaw completely. As I poked through the winter accumulation of dried weeds and grasses, there it was, a tiny lavender blue face, short stemmed, flat to the ground, a violet peeking through. The bloom could fit on the tip of my little finger. The little green leaves were no bigger than my thumb. With each spring, each first violet, comes a personal renewal. Think what joy the Pilgrims must have experienced upon seeing the tender violet after surviving their first American winter.

Look at tree branches and check the bud-plumping process. If you compare, you'll see some buds ready to burst their casings while others are "late bloomers." During your walk you might come upon a small branch or two with buds well developed. With care you might snip a twig or so to bring inside. If you are taking a "Signs of Spring Walk" in a place other than your yard, please do not cut at will in your local park or from your neighbor's yard; ask permission first. Many people are happy to share.

Redbud and plum tree branches as well as cuttings from the forsythia bush open nicely indoors. Place the cuttings in a suitable vase filled with tepid water. By bringing the branches into the warmth of your home, you are encouraging the buds to open early. Day by day examine the subtle changes in the buds. By this time you've surely noticed the similarity between tree buds and budding human development. As in all things there are early beauties and late bloomers.

If you are fortunate, you may have a brushy, uncultivated corner in your yard or a wooded lot down the street. As summer approaches and the violets are on the wane, May apples appear in wooded areas. The flat leaves look like little five- or six-inch green tables standing around several inches above the ground. Look under the green "table" and see a lovely white flower. If the time for the flower is past, little round green "May apples" appear. They are charming to see, but not to be eaten.

Depending on the location, various wildflower treasures may be found. Jack-In-The-Pulpit and Johnny Jump-Ups, as some folks call them, are great surprises as the observer gently probes through dead grasses in wooded areas. Buttercups choose sunny locations, usually in the middle of a lawn. At the edge of the woods tiny white Stars of Bethlehem bloom.

If the primal food gathering urge strikes you on your Looking for Signs of Spring Walk, try to resist all but ramps and dandelions until you have basic knowledge. Dandelion greens are mild and tender but only before the bud appears. In maturity dandelions become tough and bitter. Just as other greens, they cook down, so it takes a field of dandelion greens for a serving.

Ramps, pungent wild cousins to the onion, must be dug and cooked, not eaten raw. It is not just my observation that ramp eaters reek. Not only is the breath terrible, but ramp odor seems to exude from the pores as well. In West Virginia, ramps were a smelly fact of life. Sometimes in self defense we ate them. When we didn't eat, we showed little mercy on someone who did partake of ramps. We always threatened to send that lone ramp eater into the woods for two weeks until the stink subsided.

Some plants are fine to collect at one stage, but they can be toxic at another stage of development. Collecting mushrooms is risky. There are several published guides to edible wild foods. Your county extension agent can also be of great help.

You have been looking, but have you been listening? If you are near white and loblolly pine trees on a sunny spring day, you might hear a small clicking sound, similar to children snapping their small fingers. The gentle, barely audible snapping sound comes from pine cones drying and opening in the warmth of the sun.

A Midsummer's Night Walk

Any evening before the breathless heat of summer is good for a walk. Thoughts of Shakespeare's strange and wondrous intrigues in the enchanted forest of Titania, Oberon, and Puck turn a generic, mosquito-swatting walk into pleasurable adventure. Just as the light of day is fading behind the trees the birds do the last serious singing of the day, as if one more mighty effort will fill the air with song to linger until sunrise. As the birds wind down their songs, there is winking and blinking as the fireflies adorn the night. As you stroll past a stand of trees, feel the difference in the air temperature. Warm, cool, then warm again. It is a natural inclination to back up and recheck the cool spot.

Many flowers close as the light dwindles. Observe varieties like morning glories, four o'clocks, and day lilies, which close, and those stalwart bachelor buttons, daisies, and clovers, which bloom on through the night. Look carefully in the grass at twilight as the dew is forming on the grass and leaves. Clover leaves seem to disappear. Actually, in the evening the little leaves fold up along the middle vein and then cluster together along the stem. With the drying action and warmth of morning sun, the leaves will reopen. Another interesting growth phenomenon I have recently discovered in my yard is that every wild morning glory vine and every honeysuckle vine seem to twine in the same manner, a counter-clockwise direction.

Some people choose not to walk on summer evenings because of things gliding, buzzing and swooping around through the air. Watch the air acrobatics of winged hunters as they catch insects in mid-air. More than likely the divers and swoopers are bats. They fly by on summer evenings feeding on airborne insects, including mosquitoes. These frequently misunderstood mammals are not to be feared or exterminated. Aware of these small, shy creatures' role in insect control, an organization called Bat Conservation International is engaged in research to preserve and protect bats.

At dusk as dew drops form on the grasses, the garden snakes and turtles move about the yard and garden. Many people are repulsed and frightened by snakes; it is an all-too-common impulse to kill the "narrow fellow in the grass" of Emily Dickinson's poetic reference. It helps to be able to tell at a safe distance the venomous "fellow" from his vastly more numerous kin who are both useful, as consumers of rats and mice, and otherwise benign.

Denied the dubious pleasure of rattlesnakes, we grew up with copperheads, but only rarely did we see them. Generally, they wanted to be around us less than we wanted to be with them. Some believe, as I do, that a black snake living in a woodpile will keep rats away.

On this mid-summer evening, you might accidentally come upon a turtle feeding on blackberries, grapes, tomatoes or other fleshy items in your yard, and fat bugs drawn also to that fruitful feast. Turtles hiss, can give a nasty bite, and are best left to peacefully prowl.

About the time the birds have sung their last songs, the trees are alive with fireflies. Tree frogs, ditch frogs and crickets start the evening symphony. Clap you hands and they will stop for a moment. Still, there is no way to tune out the nocturnal frog cacophony during a wet spell in summer.

Autumn In The Air Walk

Look all around as you walk. What do you see besides changing colors? It is true, the pastels of spring and the vibrant summer colors give way to mellow earth tones, becoming John Keats' "season of mists and mellow fruitfulness." Pods are drying, wild morning glory seed heads bulge, split, and spill their contents. You might find "hitch-hikers" or burrs on your socks and pants legs. Just know those sticking, poking things, such a nuisance to pick off, are but seeds hitching a ride to another location. You, the transporter, become a backyard Johnny Appleseed.

As the breezes pass through the branches, the leaves rustle in a way that tells the listener a leaf shower is not far away. In my yard as the leaves fall, the sounds of the outside world are no longer muffled. Although the highway is some distance from my house as is the railroad crossing, the horns, whistles, and sirens, absorbed in the protective green of summer, are now distinct.

Try standing under a tree while the leaves are green and hanging tight. Clap your hands and note how the sound is muffled by the leaves. Soon the tree-cleaning storm will come. Until that point the leaves swirl and gently flutter down. Children love to watch little clusters of leaves circle-dance in mini-tornadoes across the yard. Listen during the next big storm how the autumn rain pummels the roof once it no longer passes through layers of leaves. Go back to the clapping tree once the leaves have fallen. Compare the empty tree clap to the full leaf sound. The time for raking is at hand. Peaceful weekends are interrupted with the whine of leaf blowers. Unplug and rake the leaves. Let the kids jump in the leaf piles.

The sound of raking wakens my dog Josie, no matter how good the dream, how deep the sleep. This blond Labrador retriever pounces on the leaves as the rake moves them into piles. She chases the gum balls and pine cones as if each one rolled for her personal pleasure.

Take inventory of your special area, and you will be surprised at the number of things other than leaves that also drop. Pine cones, pine tags, gum balls, and nuts hide in the grasses. You might discover little mound-like "disturbed" places in your yard. Chances are squirrels have been at work, diligently digging little holes, depositing nuts, then replacing the dirt. In all my days of squirrel watching, I have yet to see a squirrel return to the burial mound to recover the stash of nuts.

Why not collect acorns, hickory nuts, black walnuts, chestnuts or what ever nut varieties "fall" your way. Bake nuts slowly in a warm oven (200 degrees) for an hour to kill any resident worms. Save these treasures and put them out for the forgetful but grateful squirrels when winter encompasses your backyard.

On nut collecting expeditions in my backyard, my faithful Josie stays at my side. Without fail one very vocal, tail switching squirrel jumps around in the branches above us and scolds in a way that sounds very much like a fussy baby. Although there is squabbling among the squirrels and probably untold violence in the insect population, for all practical purposes, my backyard is a peaceable kingdom.

Josie, raised with a guinea pig, loves all furry things. From her place in the sun on the back porch, summer after summer she watches "yard bunny" leap the garden fence and munch rows of beans to the ground. Her nose works a little bit while yard bunny eats the tops off dandelions, but doesn't leave the porch to sniff the spot until the coast is clear. Josie holds a good point on a frog or butterfly until it moves, then she backs away.

Always include an autumn evening walk with the approaching autumnal equinox. In the cool evenings a few hearty crickets remain in song. Look carefully for blinking lights. The fireflies are nearly gone, but here and there a female glows, sheltered from the cool night deep in the grass. There are other lights in the autumn nights. Look up into the clear autumn or early winter evening sky. With the stars in their radiance, one need not be Steven Crane's "Learned Astronomer" to pick out the Big and Little Dipper and Orion the Hunter. One children's story to explain the changing of the seasons says that when animals go into hibernation, they are hiding from Orion the Hunter who stands in wait in the autumn sky.

There is one other sheer delight that mysteriously lights up the late summer and early autumn evenings. That elusive but delightful phenomenon is called foxfire. Stories are woven around this evening light which seems to appear most often after heavy, late summer rains. Biologists explain foxfire as phosphorus oxidizing in wood which contains certain types of fungi. Although I have watched for it over the years I have only seen it twice. At those times, I felt as if Nature had awarded me a special privilege. One gets a similar rush of joy when discovering a rainbow. It wasn't there, now it is, and in the twinkling of an eye it vanishes.

Bundle Up Winter Is Here

Notice the quiet during a winter walk. The air is cold, sometimes stings your nose and cheeks. Mid-day is a good time for winter walking. If it's sunny, there is warmth at midday. Even misty gray days lighten a bit from eleven to one. The point is, get out there and walk. During early morning, late afternoon, and before a storm the yard is full of feeding birds. If you observe them on a regular basis, you will see that certain birds hunt, pick and peck in ways that give them special personalities. Bird tracks are always the first in new fallen snow.

Winter is the time to investigate trees. Behold the interesting shapes. You might find a fallen branch that is in itself a miniature tree. Find a place for it in your home. Adorn it as the seasons change. Examine the bark on trees. Look at the oak with its fine, defined bark. Compare it to the pine's nugget bark. Sweet gum, persimmon, and sugar maple have their own bark personalities, yet they all have something in common. Look at the bark on the trunk's base, near the earth. It is coarse. Follow the bark patterns up the tree. See how, as the bark ascends, its texture changes, becomes smoother. Look at the skin of a person eighty years old. Does it have the texture of a baby's skin? Apply this theory to tree bark: the older you get, the more wrinkles you have.

With wood hounds fueling their wood burning stoves, your chance of finding a tree stump is good. Growth rings are interesting. When trees have growth spurts, the rings are spaced far apart. In years of drought and slow growth, the space between the rings narrows. Count the rings and see how old the tree is.

You might find a tree that is hollow inside. There is always interesting speculation as to what real or imaginary residents call the hollow home. Knock on the tree and hear the hollow sound. An amazing fact is that a hollow tree is not necessarily a dead tree. The center of a tree might be eaten away by insects, blight etc, but if the life support layer just under the bark in unharmed the tree can survive.

Carving one's initials invades the life-layer and opens a pathway for disease. Think before you tie rope or wire around trees for an extended period of time. If tight enough, the rope or wire can act as a circular knife, cutting into the living layer as the tree grows.

Examining a fallen limb, or a rotten log out by the woodpile is

entertaining. My children once called rotting logs "tuna fish trees" because the decaying wood looked to them like canned tuna. Frequently, fungus formations grow on the bark of the rotting log. In warm weather ants and other insects eat away at the wood, breaking it down. Eventually it will follow the cycle and return to the earth.

Winter Wonderland Walk

It's a day for which we all hope, the first big snow of winter. For some it may be the first snow of a lifetime. Blanketed by snow, the familiar shapes take on a certain mystery and for a little while everything is new and clean. It seems as if hope and positive attitudes blow in on the coattails of the frosty north wind. Sledders, snowball-throwers and fort builders along with snowman-creators instinctively know when it's packing snow. Two steps in fresh snow will tell you. If the snow squeaks and groans beneath your boot, it will pack well.

Packing snow is snowman snow. Begin by rolling a small ball until it is big but manageable. This is the bottom of your snow person. Roll another ball, this time a little smaller, for the middle. Finally, make a smaller ball for the head. Dig under the snow and gather objects such as rocks, pine cones, sticks, dried leaves or grasses for the face and hair. You can shape arms of snow, features on the face, feet, and any other interesting curves to individualize your snow person.

Forget about snowmen and snowball fights if the snow won't pack. Seize the opportunity to create snow graffiti! Mix a strong food coloring and water solution in a plastic pump/spray bottle. Pack a snow design the way you would sand for a sand sculpture, then spray it. Try several different colors in free form designs. If you are not satisfied with a particular artistic endeavor, heap snow on it and begin again, or move to another patch of snow.

Do you remember how to make a snow angel? You probably won't need to go far to find an untouched patch of snow in the yard or on the front walk. Lie on your back in the snow and move your arms and legs back and forth in the snow to make the wings and the dress. Once the angel is created, paint her with your snow sculpture colored water if you wish.

Have you ever made snow ice cream? It is simple to make, with a wonderful taste that cannot be duplicated. If the snow came in the night, then morning is the best time to gather it for the snow cream. Pick a time to walk before the salt, sand, and chemical trucks begin their work and before the dogs are high stepping through the snow. My grandfather took me on snow gathering walks, showing me how to brush away the top layer to get to the "pure" snow. We gathered several buckets of snow and could leave them on the porch because the temperature was too cold for icicles to form or snow to melt.

This is my family recipe for snow ice cream. In a big mixing bowl beat 1 cup of evaporated milk, 1 whole egg, 1/2 cup granulated sugar and 1 teaspoon of vanilla. Spoon the clean snow into the beaten mixture until it becomes the consistency of sherbet. Serve and eat the snow cream now or store it in a covered plastic container in the freezer.

Penny Walk

With great enthusiasm a child will begin a walk. Five minutes later, the fascination has wilted. Then it's time for a penny walk. In any season at any time of day, walk for a time in one direction, looking, listening, examining things. Flip the penny. Heads you turn to the right, tails to the left, turn around or continue forward, or whatever direction you choose. Variation: look up, then look down as you walk.

If you have several children with you, a flip of the coin could be a strategic decision-maker determining, "do we continue or do we go home?" Sometimes a change is welcome to weary legs or the shredded patience of adults. Flip the coin and ask, "A penny for your thoughts?" As the direction changes, the curiosity level goes up. A Penny Walk works well in the yard, in a field, or on a city sidewalk.

While walking, flip the penny for a cloud break. Sit down, or lie down if the area is suitable and scan the sky for cloud formations. Sometimes clouds look stacked upon each other forming pillars, towers and stately mansions. Study the clouds and see how the pictures change. If you must identify clouds, here is very basic information. For more specific information, consult the library.

Stratus and stratocumulus clouds: These are the smooth low clouds that seem to blanket the earth on gray drizzle days.

Nimbus clouds: Big, dark, billowing clouds that promise downpours and perhaps a lightning show and thunderclaps.

Cumulus and cumulonimbus clouds: Puffy, fluffy, drifting across the sky, these are the white clouds that hold many pictures among their cotton-like mounds and rounds.

Cirrus clouds: These are the delicate, feathery high flying clouds which reside at the "top" of the sky. These clouds are not made of water drops as the others are. They are composed of ice crystals. The moisture ring that sometimes rims the moon is actually a cirrostratus cloud.

Identifying specific types of clouds is interesting, but has absolutely no bearing on where your imagination takes you in cloud art. In cloud formations, without fail my son Sandy spots at least one "Honest Abe Lincoln" profile. Occasionally he sees some four legged leviathan making its way across the horizon. Cloud formations change quickly, new pictures form, old ones reshape. Sometimes the clouds are the furrows of a freshly plowed field. Sunset paints exquisite cloud-colors. How long has it been since you indulged in cloud art?

The Too Tired To Walk Walk

The day is hot and everyone is grumpy. Socks are quitters, as Sandy refers to socks that slip down over heels and wad in one's

shoes. Toes are screaming to be free. In the real world of glass slivers, thorns, and stinging things, walking barefoot is hazardous. Still, splashing through puddles feels so good on bare feet.

What is there in the backyard for tired feet to do? Locate a grass-less area, perhaps the corner of the garden or flower bed. Scoop out some loose dirt to make a bowl in the ground big enough for one foot or two. Fill a bucket with water. Use a measuring cup to ladle the water from the bucket to the bare earth. Cup by cup, gently pour the water into the scooped-out area. Put one or two feet in the growing mud puddle. Add dirt if necessary to make a pasty, gooey mess. Wiggle toes. Feel the mud goo squish between the toes.

As the water soaks into the ground, the mud becomes the right consistency for mud pies, mud balls, and mud worms. Take mud and roll it around on your palms. See what a smooth ball it makes? Are you reminded of Indians and pottery and beads?

Smack the mud ball into a pancake or tortilla on the palm of your hand. Add a drop or two of water from the bucket and roll that mud into a snake or worm. Use the water in the bucket to wash your feet and hands. Water the tomatoes or flowers with the leftover mud water.

Note: water is a precious resource. Consider our earth. Don't hook up the hose and let it run. If you need more water, fill the bucket again.

Gathering and Collecting

Now that you have revived the gentle art of observation, it is time to move toward collecting. Remember there is a vast difference between collecting and making a collection. In down-to-earth terms, collecting is gathering all sorts of things that strike your fancy as you happen on them during your walk.

A collection is generally restricted to varieties of one particular thing: rocks, butterflies, flowers, shells, seeds etc. that are mounted, labeled, and displayed. Gathering is spontaneous fun and can be the first step to a collection. Collecting is a long term commitment requiring time, a degree of maturity, patience, organization, a manual or field guide, and mounting materials and a case to protect or store the collection.

In this section are many simple ideas suggesting activities to do with things gathered. I have deliberately omitted labeling the activities as suitable for this age or that. With four children and their friends I have always had mixed ages around my kitchen table and in my backyard. It has been my experience that the older ones help the younger children. There is a feeling of togetherness rather than sibling rivalry. In a non-competitive, cooperative atmosphere, everybody feels success. Sometimes older children actually find it a relief to toss aside teenage-itis and be young again. You must use your good judgment. The first, second or even third attempt at togetherness may not be what you consider successful. Resist that need to get out the fun barometer or evaluate the amount learned. Those are omnipresent pitfalls. Consider yourself and those with you pilgrims in search of fun. Relax, have a good time, and know that the trip along the way might be as pleasant and entertaining as actually reaching the destination.

Through general gathering, an interest in a specific area may develop. Then is the time to begin a collection. There is no quicker turnoff to a child than to be overwhelmed. Think how often we overanswer the questions children ask us and wonder at the same time why they aren't listening after the first sentence. To keep it simple is to offer incentive for further investigation.

Leaf Gathering

Whenever possible gather freshly fallen leaves. Sometimes it becomes necessary to pick. Be gentle to the tree or plant as you pick or snip. Try never to break off branches or take more than you can use.

Examine each leaf for its secret identity. Run your finger along the veins, the lifeline of the leaves. Some leaves have a large vein sort of like a back bone that goes up the center of the leaf. Smaller symmetrical veins branch out from the central vein looking a bit like the backbone with ribs. Other leaves have a central vein that branches to smaller veins. The smaller veins have tiny veins which feather out like back roads traveling in various directions to the farthest points and lobes of the leaves.

There are leaves with points and slightly jagged edges like sweet gum, sycamore, or sugar maple. Some leaves like the horse chestnut and slippery elm that have "saw-tooth edges." Redbud and tulip poplar leaves are smooth edged, as are sassafras leaves which resemble mittens. Consider plant leaves in addition to tree leaves. As you develop an interest or mount leaves for a scrapbook, use an official field guide for specific information, common name, botanical name, location, etc. In the beginning consider the shape, color, size and texture before concerning yourself with identification.

Often there are smooth little lumps and fuzzy big bumps on leaves. These formations created by insects laying eggs within the tissues of the leave are called galls. These are not the same thing as cocoons. Galls are abnormal tissue growth on the leaf. When a gall is about the size of the tip of a little finger, usually there is an insect inside that can be closely examined with the magnifying glass. Use a small knife to gently open the little insect home, if you are curious as to exactly who resides within.

Leaf Boat Races

This is pre-raking fall activity for when the leaves are dry and curled. Select any large dry leaf which has begun to curl up. Oak leaves work nicely as do sweet gum and maple. It is best to have moving water, such as a stream, swale or ditch. Determine the starting point and an end point for the race and station people there. One person releases the boats while the other waits down stream at the finish line. Participants may wish to release their own boats and run to the finish line. Huff and puff, blowing the leaves along in a ditch race.

My children recall leaf and stick races at "Gran's" in West Virginia. They enjoyed tossing leaves or sticks off one side of the little bridge and running to the other side to see whose item passed from under the bridge first. It was usually my son Matt's fortune to wait and wait because without fail one leaf or stick, always his, was detained under the bridge. To be sure there was always good five or ten minute investigation and speculation on how the mishap occurred. Was it the time of release, position of item at time of release, change in current? No conclusions were ever drawn, just more items tossed into the moving creek.

Four children of assorted ages tossing leaves and sticks into a creek didn't change the course of world events. What did happen was the delightful sound of children's laughter in the air, time together, and memories.

Leaf Rubbings
MATERIALS:
Fresh leaf
Thin paper such as typing or duplicating paper (white or colored)
Colored crayon

Directions: Place a leaf, dry of dew, raindrops or other moisture, face down on a hard, flat surface so the prominent veins on the underside are up. Cover the leaf with the typing paper. Peel the wrapping off crayon. Do not use the tip of the crayon. Place the length of the crayon on the paper; rub gently back and forth over the leaf. Soon the image of the leaf will appear.

Hint: Begin in a simple way with one leaf. You may wish to move to a sophisticated leaf design with several leaves of the same type or an assortment of sizes and shapes. Plan out your design on another paper before you begin. Consult your pattern as you rub. Rub one leaf at a time. If you try to place all the leaves, cover and rub at the same time, the leaves will shift and frustration will outweigh the joy of doing.

Leaf Prints
MATERIALS:
> Fresh leaf or leaves
> Manila or other construction paper ·
> Ink or tempera paint, or water-base latex interior flat-wall paint (Please consider our environment. Refuse to be tempted by paint in aerosol cans!)
> Small roller or 1/2-inch width trim brush
> Paint pan (pie pan, cake tin etc.)
> Newspaper
> Paper towels

Directions: Cover the work surface with newspaper. Inspect the leaves to make sure they are fresh, flexible and moisture free. With paper toweling, gently pat the leaves being careful not to bruise or tear them. Place the leaf face up on the newspaper. Place a small amount of paint in utility pan. With the roller or brush cover the leaf with paint.

Carefully place the art paper on top of the ink-or-paint-covered leaf and apply firm steady pressure for about 15 seconds.

Lift the art paper directly up and quickly turn it over. For best success without telltale runs don't use the "peek and peel back" motion. Drips and runs are common if the artist has been generous with the paint. Clean up the newspaper and wash paint materials in warm soapy water.

Hint: Save a roll-top deodorant bottle. Remove the top and wash the bottle and roll top until completely free of chemical residue. Fill the bottle 3/4 full with paint and replace the roll top. You have done your part in recycling, saved money and avoided an ink or paint mess.

Variation: Why not try a reverse print? Put the leaf on the art paper. Roll paint over the entire paper including the leaf. Carefully, remove the leaf.

Leaf Print On A Tee Shirt
MATERIALS:
Leaf for printing
Indelible ink (colors are available at craft and art stores)
Roller or brush
Ink pan
100% cotton tee shirt, white or color
Newspaper
Paper towels
Soft cardboard or blotter paper
Straight pins

Directions: Spread newspaper. Place small amount of ink in pan or in roll-top bottle. Spread the shirt flat on a covered work surface. Slip the cardboard inside the shirt between the front and back so the ink won't leak through the shirt. If possible, pin the shirt at the shoulders, on the arms, under the arms and across the bottom onto the work surface so the shirt won't move as the leaf is placed on it.

Pat the leaf with a paper towel to remove any excess moisture. Evenly spread ink over the leaf. Position the leaf on the shirt. Cover the leaf with paper towel and press down with even pressure for about sixty seconds. A catalog, magazine or book is good to use. Remove the magazine, paper towel, and leaf. Let the shirt dry undisturbed overnight. To avoid fading or running, soak the shirt (after the 24 hours drying period) in warm salt water. Use one-half cup of salt for every one gallon of water.

Leaf Print By Spatter Painting
MATERIALS:
8" X 8" square of fine mesh screen wire
Silver duct tape or 2-inch wide electrical tape
Construction paper
Toothbrush
Leaves
Tempera paint (one color or assorted colors)
Paint pan
Two bricks or scrap wood
Newspaper

Directions: Bind the edges of the screen by folding the tape evenly over the mesh. This will create a box-like effect which will eventually appear as an even, unpainted border around the print. Spread the work surface with newspaper. Place the construction paper on the prepared surface. Place a fresh, clean, moisture-free leaf on the construction paper. If the artist wants a design of several leaves, now is the time to position all the leaves.

Position the bricks or wood so the prepared screening when resting on these props is just above the leaves.

While holding the screen steady with one hand, dip the brush in the paint with the other hand. Gently brush back and forth across the mesh. In this case, the less paint used the better. Globs can form in the mesh and drop down onto the paper. When changing colors either use another brush or thoroughly wash the brush in warm sudsy water. Dry the bristles and continue painting. When the painting is completed, remove the screening and the leaves. The leaf outlines remain set on a finely-spattered background.

Variation: This project works well for very young children. Eliminate the brick supports and lay the screening with its taped edges directly on the leaf and paper. Proceed as above. Gently remove screen and leaves.

Leaf Fossils
MATERIALS:
> Leaf
> Plaster of Paris
> 1 cup cold water
> Small mixing bowl
> Cooking oil
> 3", 4" or 6" plastic lid
> Paper towels
> Newspaper

Directions: Spread a newspaper base on your work area. Choose interesting leaves with prominent features to "fossilize." The artist should not be limited to one leaf or one mold.

Select a plastic lid from a soft drink mix can, coffee can, margarine tub, etc. and use the side of the lid which has the recessed area and higher lip. Each lid is different. Sometimes the underside is better than top side.

Dab a minimal amount of cooking oil on a paper towel and gently wipe across the lid surface. The lid should not appear oily. Pat the leaf to clean it and remove any moisture. With the same paper toweling used to lubricate the plastic lid, gently wipe the side of the leaf with prominent veins. This will be the side that makes the fossil impression in the plaster of Paris.

Position the leaf in the lid. Fill the small mixing bowl with cold water. Slowly sprinkle or sift plaster into the water-filled bowl until the water is saturated with plaster. The saturation point is when the plaster stays on top of the water. Resist the temptation to stir. After the water can hold no more plaster, hold the bowl with one hand and stick the other hand in the plaster and water and slowly stir until smooth.

Slowly pour the plaster into the lid, covering the leaf. Allow the plaster to set up over night. Gently pop the fossil out of the lid mold. Remove the leaf, and behold your fossil!

Hint: This is a messy project, but by careful covering of your work surface, cleanup is easy and everyone will be happy. After all, that's what soap and water are for. Wash the utensil and yourself immediately, because you are working with plaster, and it does harden. Recycle the plastic tubs from frozen whipped topping. The tops are good molds, while the tubs are ideal for mixing bowls.

Leaf Decorated Placemats
MATERIALS:
Leaves, assorted sizes and shapes, green or in autumn colors
Colored tissue paper
Rubber cement
White "poster board weight" paper
Clear self-adhesive paper
Scissors
Paper towels
Waxed paper
Brick or heavy book

Directions: Rinse fresh leaves in cool water. Pat fresh leaves on both sides to remove remaining dirt particles and moisture. Remove thick stems that might "bump up" through the self-adhesive surface.

Cut paper in desired placemat size and shape; oval is an attractive shape. However, if you are a beginner or are working with a beginner, rectangle is the easiest to cover with the clear self-adhesive paper.

Arrange leaves but do not glue down. Cut colored tissue paper in giant leaves or curved free-form as a background. Place the colored tissue behind the leaves. Overlapping the colors makes an interesting background. Now, before gluing, is the time to adjust the tissue and the leaves.

Brush the paper glue (rubber cement) on small sections of poster board. The joy of paper glue is that it dries quickly, and the excess can be gently rubbed away. The drying speed necessitates working with one small section at a time.

Gently place the tissue over the glued area. Pat and smooth it to eliminate air bubbles and wrinkles in the tissue. Glue the leaves in place on and around the tissue. Let the placemat dry for about 15 minutes, then cover it with waxed paper and weight it with a book or brick. Press the leaf design for 24 hours.

Measure and cut the clear self-adhesive paper so on all four sides it is one inch larger than the placemat. Peel off the protective covering and apply to first one side then the other side of the placemat. Smooth the clear plastic as you apply it and trim the excess from the edges.

Hint: Apply the plastic to the underside of the placemat first. Start at one end and work to the other smoothing as you go, peeling back if necessary to eliminate a wrinkle. Pesky air pockets are easily eliminated by carefully sticking a straight pin in the edge of the little blister.

Variation: 4" X 4" squares decorated with colored tissue and one leaf make good coasters. These coasters given individually or packaged in groups of six or eight squares tied with yarn or brown jute make a good gift.

Flower Gathering

Cultivated flower gardens are spectacular. The organization and profusion of colors draw attention. Each variety stands in stately grandeur vying for attention of passers-by. Each community has its share of green thumb people whose yards reflect careful planning and much hard work. While yards and gardens are in full bloom, even pessimists have a sense that all is well.

Perhaps you've discovered as I have, with personal joy, a secret garden, a place where the wild things bloom. Surprisingly, little wildflowers which appear so delicate are quite hardy and can be preserved as well as cultivated flowers. By all means in your gathering, resist clipping the little species endangered or in short supply. It isn't likely that we will ever make a dent in the supply of violets and buttercups, so pick away and enjoy.

Flowering imagination

The test: Have you taken or given the ageless, perennial "Do You Like Butter" test recently? Hold a buttercup beneath someone's chin. If there is a golden reflection, this is proof positive the subject likes butter. Although toddlers catch on right away to the buttercup test, they are less discriminating than older children about picking. You may find yourself being tested by a toddler clutching a hand full of grass and buttercups. Examining and selecting just the right buttercup for the test was always part of the fun for my children. Every family that participates in the testing has a resident buttercup authority. Jenny, my only daughter, was the self-appointed buttercup authority among her three brothers as they were growing up.

The big bite: A special children's flower is the Snapdragon. These are tall, profuse clusters of bright color in the garden. Some are solid ruby, yellow, or pink. Some are hybrids, salmon pink with shades of rose, yellow with deep orange. No matter what the colors, snapdragons have one thing in common, they snap. Gently remove one bloom from the stalk. Pinch the sides and watch the little mouth open. Children are intrigued, looking down the little snapdragon throat. All kinds of pretend games are possible. The least imaginative is, "Say...Ah...." when the child assumes the doctor or dentist persona peering into the mouth. The little blooms become tiny puppets, talking away as the mouths open and close. It seems as if there is always one child who prefers to have the snapdragon bite. (This seems to be the same personality that makes hand puppets bite.)

He loves me: Think twice before you pull up wild daisies which have made their weedy way into your garden. Just how hard is it to revive that heart throb game, "He Loves Me, He Loves Me Not?" Remember that first crush? You couldn't get the nerve to speak to the person, but you surely could pluck the petals from the daisy to see if this were true love. Pick the first petal, "he loves me." The second petal, "he loves me not." To find out your romantic future work your way around the daisy pulling petals, alternating "loves me," and "loves me not" until all the petals are plucked.

Make a wish: As the yellow dandelions go to seed, they become puff balls. These puff balls are a menace to a gardener but a delight to children. The rule of thumb says that in order to have a wish come true, the wisher must be able to pick the dandelion puff ball without disturbing a single "puff." If the wisher is able to accomplish the picking challenge, he or she must then make a silent wish, take a very deep breath, and blow all the puffs from the stem in a single breath.

Clover Jewelry

Before the lawnmower levels the clover in the back yard make a clover tiara, necklace and matching bracelet. The jewelry is made by varying the length of clover chains. Come on, think back, surely you made a clover chain! I spent my 11th summer trying to make the world's longest clover chain. It stretched clear across the road and doubled back again. I kept it wrapped in a moist dishtowel in the refrigerator. Perhaps, the chain had reached its peak and was gradually doing that thing that old clover chains do; however, I believe to this day it was the neighbor's blue pickup truck backing over it that was the final crushing blow.

The way to have an outstanding clover chain is to pick the clover, leaving as much stem as possible. Wrap a stem of one clover just under the head of a second clover. Tie a knot in the stem just below the head of a second clover. Repeat this stem wrapping and knotting process until the chain is as long as you want. Turn it into a circle by tying the last stem around the head of the first clover.

In those days of endless clover supply my neighbor, Mark, was able to shoot the clover heads into the air by tying the stem of a clover in a loop just beneath the head. In one fluid motion, he could move the knot forward as he tightened it and send the head flying. He always had a personal clover head best-distance he was trying to beat.

If you have the good fortune to have a supply of daisies, you can make daisy chain jewelry. Violets can be used also. As you pick violets, choose ones with hardy stems. The delicate stems bruise and won't tie a satisfactory knot.

Drying Flowers

Growing and preserving flowers are wonderful "inter-generational" activities. Little ones enjoy the gathering, counting, tying, and hanging flowers to dry. Measuring the string and cutting it are important activities. Binding the stems and finding just the right location to hang the bundles take on ceremonial tones. Looking to the practical aspect, the brief preparation time interests those with attention spans of gnats.

Children age 10 and older seem to enjoy the process of burying, checking, and retrieving the flowers from the drying medium. They show interest in detail and are gentle, willing to take time to filter the powder among the petals and then when the flowers are dry, delicately brush away the residue.

Pressing flowers has to be the all time favorite of young and old. The materials are few, and the results are charming. If ever there were a conversation-producing activity, this is it. As the hands work with the delicate blossoms, something happens within. Workers share with and listen to each other. Suddenly Grandma has stories to which everyone listens. Maybe Mother and daughter talk without being at odds. In brief harmony Big Sister and Little Brother work together.

After collecting flowers and surveying the interest level of your helpers, decide in which manner you would like to preserve your bouquet. Consider various ways to dry and preserve for lasting arrangements and interesting craft projects before you choose your method. As you ponder the possibilities, examine the complete flower. Your time, personal dedication and enthusiasm, as well as the thickness of petal, texture, color and eventual use will help you determine the best method.

The Hanging Method

This is a partial list of vegetation which dries exceptionally well using this method:

Baby's breath	Self-heal heads
Cock's comb	Straw flower
Dusty miller leaves	Tansy buttons
German statice	Wild grasses
Hydrangea blooms	Zinnia

Directions: Gather six flowers and tie the stems together with yarn or string. Hang in a cool, dry place out of direct sunlight. This method takes 3 to 4 weeks depending upon the drying conditions and the moisture level in the plant.

Hint: Cut the stems from zinnias and straw flowers. Insert floral wire into the flower heads for a sturdy stem to use in arrangements.

Uses: Dried flowers can be arranged in a doily and tied with ribbon streamers for a child's bouquet. Clusters of dried flowers tied with ribbon can be pinned to drapery tie-backs for decoration. Stemless flowers can be glued across the top of a painted clip board. Other stemless flowers can be arranged and glued the tops of small straw or wooden boxes to be used as treasure boxes or decorative boxes on dressers. Save the flowers which didn't dry well to make your own potpourri.

The Borax Or Silica Gel Method

The best way to know what dries best is to try drying everything that strikes your fancy. This is a partial list of vegetation that dries well in preservatives:

Asters	Daisies
Bachelor buttons	Larkspur
Carnations	Rose buds

MATERIALS:
Silica gel OR 3 cups powdered borax
3 cups white cornmeal
Floral wire
Large wide mouth container with tight-fitting lid. (Deep, 1-gallon plastic frozen yogurt or ice cream containers work well.)
Flowers for drying

Directions: You can't really go wrong using silica gel because drying items in finely crushed silica gel crystals ensures retention of brilliant colors. It is available at craft stores or florist supply stores. But it is usually my choice to use what I have on hand rather than rushing to the store to buy materials. To make a suitable drying medium, combine 2 cups of powdered borax and 2 cups of white cornmeal.

Select a flower, remove stem and leaves. Insert floral wire into the flower head to provide a sturdy stem for future use in a dried arrangement. Fill the container with about 4 inches of the drying medium. Double over the wire if necessary as you insert the flower, head up into the mixture. Make sure the cornmeal/borax combination filters through all the petals. Otherwise, some moisture might remain and later on mildew could develop.

Place several flowers in this layer. Cover with the drying medium. If the container is deep enough you could dry a second layer of flowers. Probably you will not need to bend the wire stems for additional layers.

Make sure each layer is completely covered; top with about two more inches of the cornmeal/borax mixture. Put on the cover, set aside and let dry for 6-7 days. Test for dryness. The flowers should have a papery but not brittle texture. If moisture remains, simply put the flower back in the powder and let dry a few more days. When all flowers are completely dry, remove them one at a time, blowing, shaking or gently dusting with a watercolor paint brush to remove any excess drying medium.

Encourage a child to assemble a simple yet attractive arrangement of home dried flowers displayed under a glass dome. Arrange the flowers, holding them in place by inserting the stems in clay on a wooden base. After the arrangement is completed, cover the clay with Spanish moss. Put the glass dome over the arrangement.

Pressing Flowers

This form of flower preservation reached its prime in mid-19th century England but seems to be regaining momentum. During the Victorian era flowers were an integral part of personal and public life. Queen Victoria lived in a manner considered by many as straight laced and severely proper, but she enjoyed flowers. Fashionable women mirrored the queen's botanical interests. They even went so far as to send and receive messages through bouquets of flowers. Friendships were initiated or nipped in the bud depending on the types of flowers sent or received. People of all ages are amazed and intrigued by the language of flowers. Some classic examples are:

Daisy   innocence
Pansy   happy thoughts
Rose   love
Violet   modesty

Flowers suitable for pressing:
Delphinium   Pansy
Geranium (individual blooms)   Violet
Hydrangea (individual blooms)

MATERIALS:
Flowers, leaves of good color, interesting shapes, veins etc.
Blotting paper or waxed paper
Masking tape
Large book, out-of-date telephone directory or catalog
Heavy weight such as a brick

Directions: Make sure your flowers are completely dry, free of insects, specks of dirt, and blemishes. Each item to be pressed, whether it is flower or leaf, must be "perfectly" perfect. Plan to press more than you need for projects in case some items mildew, fade too badly or just plain don't dry well.

On a sheet of waxed paper or blotting paper smooth out leaves and arrange flower petals etc. so that they are straight and flat. If you dry more than one item on a paper, leave plenty of space between them. Cover with a second piece of waxed or blotting paper.

Cut a strip of masking tape and place it on the outside of the paper. Write the date and the name of specimen. Whether or not you identify what you are drying is not an integral part of the process. It is for your personal information and reflection. The date is of assistance when you are determining just how long this specimen has been tucked away.

Carefully slide the little package into the book you have chosen for your "flower press." Select a warm, out-of-the-way corner for the pressing as it takes about 6 weeks. Weight down the book with the brick or a stack of books.

Don't even consider taking a quick look at how the pressing is going. You can ruin the specimen by letting air and light in while you are peeking.

Hint: For best results try not to mix thicknesses. The pressure will be uneven and the drying will not be as successful.

Pressed Flower Gifts

There are many lovely and elegant gifts that can be made using pressed flowers. Trays, pictures and other delights remind us of gracious Victorian times. If you develop an artist's interest in this long-ago craft, you can move to more sophisticated projects. The very basic ideas suggested here are to reacquaint you, to introduce children to the art and most of all, to keep it pocketbook friendly.

Note Pad
MATERIALS:
Note pad, unlined, white or colored paper
Pressed flowers
Clear self adhesive paper
Scissors
White glue thinned with water
Toothpick

Glue dish
Small watercolor brush

Directions: Measure and cut a piece of self adhesive paper to cover the front and back of the note pad. Select the pressed flowers and arrange. Use the paintbrush to push the delicate pressed flowers into position. This way you avoid the possibility of damaging petals or spreading the natural oil from your hands when touching the flowers.

Use the glue sparingly. A tiny dot of glue on the end of a tooth pick spread gently on one petal should be sufficient for each flower. When the flowers are glued down, let them dry for an hour. Cover with contact paper, beginning at the bottom front edge and working towards the back. Make sure this is a smooth fit without wrinkles or air blisters. The little flowers are so fragile that they will break apart if the adhesive paper is pulled up and reapplied.

Bookmark
MATERIALS:
2" X 6" piece of typing paper or construction paper
Pressed flowers
White glue thinned with water
Glue dish
Toothpick
Clear self adhesive paper
Watercolor paint brush

Directions: Follow the directions for making the pressed flower note pad.

Stationery
MATERIALS:
Blank fold over note cards and envelopes
Pressed flowers
White glue thinned with water
Glue dish
Toothpick
Watercolor paint brush
Gold cord
Clear self adhesive paper

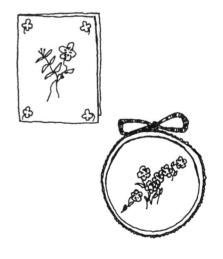

Directions: On the front of the note card in the center arrange pressed flowers in an oval position. Use the note pad directions for placing and gluing flowers. Cut an oval of adhesive paper slightly larger than the design. After the glue has dried peel the protective backing off the adhesive paper and put over the design.

Glue the gold cord around the edge of the clear plastic to conceal the edge.

Hint: It is best not to cut the cord until you have completed the gluing process. Many a length of cord can be wasted by being cut too short.

Dyeing With Flowers

"Stewing" up a kettle of flowers to make fabric dye is quick and fun. Check with the produce manager at your local grocery. He will certainly keep you supplied with bags of onion skins. Here are some of the most common backyard and garden materials for dye:

Yellow:	Goldenrod flowers, yarrow flowers, dandelion heads
Gold:	Marigold heads, skins of yellow onions
Orange:	Sunflower, skins of red onions
Tan:	Raspberries
Green:	Bayberry
Purple:	Blackberries, elderberries, or grapes
Gray:	Poplar bark
Black:	Black walnut husks

MATERIALS:
Flowers (4-6 cups)
Fruits or nuts (8 ounces)
2 3-4 gallon kettles
Stirring stick
Plastic colander
Small scale (diet or postage scale works)
2 ounces powdered alum
1/2 ounce cream of tartar
2 gallons of water
Rubber glove

Directions for making the dye: When using outer hulls of nuts or crushed berries, soak overnight in 1 gallon of water. Strain the contents and reserve the soaking water. If using berries or hulls put 1 gallon of fresh water and the reserved soaking water into a large kettle. When working with fresh flowers use 2 gallons of water.

Add the nuts, berries, chopped leaves or flowers and bring the mixture to a boil, then simmer for 45 minutes, stirring occasionally.

Stir in the alum and cream of tartar. This mixture is a color enhancer. Flower dyes are not as bold as commercial chemical dyes. Let the mixture cool to room temperature before using.

General dyeing directions: Use fabric that is 100% cotton. You may want to begin by dyeing a piece of cotton string or thread. Consider recycling worn out cotton bed sheets into dyeing squares, head or neck scarves, colorful sashes to tie around the middle.

Rinse the fabric to be dyed in lukewarm water and wring out excess water. Put the fabric in the dye kettle. Slowly warm the dye on medium heat until it reaches a simmer. Stir occasionally and lift the fabric to check the color. Whenever the fabric is the color you like, the dyeing is complete. Flower dye takes about a half an hour. The nut and bark dyes take from one to two hours.

Rinse the hot fabric in warm water until the water is clear.

Rinse the fabric in lukewarm water mixed with 1/2 cup white vinegar or salt to set the color.

Tie-Dyeing A Tee Shirt The Natural Way

MATERIALS:
> 100% cotton tee shirt
> Rubber bands
> Natural dye
> Large kettle

Directions: Follow the directions for preparing dye. Grasp a handful of shirt and bind the fabric with a rubber band (4-6 twists of the rubber band around the fabric). Repeat this as many times and in as many places around the shirt as you wish.

Use lukewarm water to wet a 100% cotton tee shirt. Put the damp shirt into the lukewarm dye kettle. Increase the heat and follow the dyeing directions. Follow the post-dyeing instructions to set the color. As you become more experienced at tie dyeing, try preparing and using several colors.

Variation 1: Make one giant twist in the middle of the front and in the middle of the back for a spiral effect.

Variation 2: For a linear tie-dye look, fold the entire shirt in fan pleats. Bind with 6 or 7 rubber bands placed at intervals the length of the folded shirt.

Rocking Fun

On every walk it is a given that children kick and pick up stones. Some children believe that the only possible activity involved with a rock after looking at it is throwing it at a dog, bird, cyclist, or other unfortunate moving or stationary target.

On Saturdays, my grandfather asked me to collect and scrub white "lucky stones" from our gravel driveway at Frog Hollow. He then put the stones in the stew pot with chopped chives, parsley and chicken bouillon and produced a most delicious, steaming broth. The rocks were strained from the broth as it was ladled into the bowls.

I loved my grandfather's "rock soup." I also believed in and carried a lucky stone from the driveway at Frog Hollow. Long after I moved from the farm, I had comfort and security with that smooth, oddly oval, translucent rock in my pocket.

There was some secret understanding of rocks we all had as kids. We knew which made good skipping stones, instinctively recognized soft writing stones. The disliked boy in the neighborhood always claimed to have flint "back at the house." We never saw it, and never gave up testing rocks hoping to find the one from which the sparks flew.

During the spring plowing, occasionally we found Indian arrow heads. A find of arrow heads always set off a rash of behind-the-shed relentless rock hammering and grinding by those without arrow heads, but hoping to produce reasonable facsimiles. Each plowing season we spent afternoons under the trees speculating about setting up an arrow head business and making huge profits to support us for a lifetime. No matter the time or place rocks are still fun.

Skipping Stones

Find a small flat stone no bigger than a quarter. The stone does not have to round, but it must be flat and thin. You will need a puddle, water-filled drainage ditch, pond, creek, river etc.

Hold the skipping stone between your thumb and forefinger. With a flick of the wrist, fling it sidearm style, not over hand or under hand.

The stone should skip across the water's surface at least twice. My sons Chris and Matt have mastered the technique so that stones literally dance across the water with seven, eight, sometimes nine skips. This is a mesmerizing activity on a summer afternoon or evening.

Rock Painting

Nice flat rocks three to five inches long lend themselves to painting. The rule of thumb should be, the smaller the artist, the bigger the rock. Older children and adults have developed the manual dexterity to paint in small detail. Young children may enjoy painting the rock...literally. Not painting a picture on it, just covering the rock with paint. A satisfying activity for younger children is to paint the rock a solid color and apply a decal or sticker when the paint is dry. Never insult or distract the artist at work by asking what he or she is painting. A time honored, honest response to a big green or blue rock which has worked for me is, "With your permission, I'd like to use this as a paper weight (door stop if it is a huge rock). Every time I look at this, I will think of you." That truthful statement usually brings a smile and a private sense of "thank goodness she knows what this is because I haven't quite figured it out yet" relief within the artist.

Rock Pets

Let imagination take flight and create fantasy forms from assorted rocks.

MATERIALS:
> Rocks in various sizes
> White craft glue
> Movable eyes
> Model paint
> Paint brush
> Newspaper

Directions: Spread newspaper on the work surface. Paint rocks in assorted colors, make stripes, polka dots, zig zag lines. Let the paint dry before handling. Select two painted rocks, one for a head and the other for a body. Glue the rocks together. Glue movable eyes to rock head. Let dry for 6-8 hours.

Variation: Turn the painted rock/friend into a refrigerator magnet by adding a self-stick magnetic tape.

Rock Turtle Paper Weight
MATERIALS:

Flat rock about the size of a silver dollar
5 small oval rocks for head and legs
Movable eyes
Felt
Scissors
White craft glue
Glue dish
Paper plate

Directions: Use the paper plate as the work surface. Put felt on the plate. Position the flat "body" rock on the felt. Arrange the 4 legs on the sides of the body. Trace around the rock turtle. Cut the felt pattern to be just a little smaller than the stones. Draw a small thin tail. On the finished turtle, the tail will remain felt, not be covered with a rock.

Pour a small amount of craft glue into the dish. Return the felt pattern to the plate. Dip the bottom of the body stone in glue and put it on the felt. Dip the legs in glue and place them on the felt. Make sure at the point the legs touch the body, there is plenty of glue. Dip the tip of the head into the glue and hold for a few minutes in the desired head position. The artist with great lung capacity may choose to blow on the glue to expedite the drying process.

Check the turtle appendages after 3 or 4 hours. If more glue is required, don't move the turtle, just dab the glue onto the spot that isn't sticking too well. Let the turtle dry for 24 hours; glue the movable eyes to the head.

Variation: To have a colorful turtle, paint the parts before gluing.

The Crown Jewels, Almost

Older children, teens especially, and adults enjoy polishing rocks. No this isn't a "done by hand" project. It requires a small investment in a rock polisher which can be purchased at most hobby shops and craft stores. The results are amazing when the rocks with ridges and pointed edges come out looking smooth and gem-like. Jewelry settings for rings, earrings, necklaces, stick pins, brooches and bracelets can be purchased at any craft store. As an economy measure, take the polished stone or stones with you so your can select settings that are the right size, style etc. for the stone. Many settings have prongs that grip the stone. Although the idea of glue on a precious gem might give you a twinge, do consider glue as backup support for the prongs holding the polished stones. Any craft supply store will have a clear, quick bond glue.

Keeping A Journal

Why keep a journal anyway? It's just another thing to nag at your conscience when you neglect making entries. Maybe it's just another thing that you invest in the materials only to have the child lose interest in less than a week. Remember? The idea is to stick to the simple things, remain unplugged!

But some will enjoy recording observations and discoveries and sometimes the thoughts of others. Pictures or sketches may be added. Pressed petals of a special flower are sometimes mounted on a page. And most will find great fun in looking back months and years later on moments and details otherwise forgotten.

A journal may be general or thematic. My daughter Jenny is interested in violent weather, and before she realized what was happening, her weather journal was well under way. In the Tidewater region of Virginia she made journal entries through droughts, floods, northeasters, hurricanes, and tornadoes. She has written of cabin cruisers dashed to toothpicks on the rocks and collected pictures of stilt houses plunging into the ocean.

Now that she lives in the mountains of North Carolina, Jenny has added blizzard entries into her journal. She experienced several snowbound days intently listening as a local radio station served as the lifeline to those isolated by the blizzard. Motorists marooned on the Blue Ridge Parkway called in by car phone requesting permission to break into a school for shelter. Jenny saved clippings of snowshoed rescuers landing by helicopter on a deserted mall parking lot and made note of Jello marks in the snow signaling need for emergency medical assistance.

In her book, *An Island Garden*, Celia Thaxter records the events through one growing season in her island garden off the coast of New Hampshire. This daughter of a lighthouse keeper speaks of reviving a hummingbird caught in a chilling north wind, of waking knowing the garden was under siege by slugs.

Some journals are an elegant combination of pictures and words such as *The Country Diary of an Edwardian Lady* by Edith Holdon. This is an enjoyable through-the-seasons book combining observations, personal thoughts, sketches, lines of poetry, all relating to the things she observed, in that age.

How you or your fledglings keep journals is a matter of personal preference. Hopefully, these suggestions will help to keep the cost down and the interest level up.

The Journal
MATERIALS:
   3-ring notebook binder
   Hole punch
   Lined paper
   Blank paper
   Paper glue
   Reinforcements
   Scissors
How To Keep A Nature Journal

The only serious "have to" in keeping a journal is to include the date of entry. Knowing date, time, and place will be a source of pleasure in years to come as you and others look through this simple treasure and reflect on special times.

What do you think about when you are walking? Write it down when your get home. Have you found a poem or a quotation that satisfies? Copy it into your journal. Is there a special picture to clip before the magazine goes in the recycle bin? Snip the picture and glue it onto a page.

Can you draw? Do you want to try to draw or do you, like so many of us, have a specialty – one thing like a five petal flower or a bare branch tree which you draw over and over? Do you doodle insects or stars and moons? Possibilities are endless. Enter your thoughts on the discovery of a seed mix the birds love or loath. Did you outwit a squirrel or watch a spider spin a web? Did you see ants in a line carrying away minute pieces of sweet roll? Did a fly buzz or a mosquito whine in your ear and you thought of all kinds of ways to stop the noise but were too tired to get out of bed?

Record these thoughts.

Have you used nature-inspired music like Antonio Vivaldi's *The Four Seasons* or Ottorino Respighi's *The Pines of Rome*, Aaron Copland's *Appalachian Spring* or Ferde Grofe's *Grand Canyon Suite* to inspire writing? Journal entries may be humorous, sensitive, serious. Incorporate poetry, prose, and a spontaneous bit of fiction.

A three-ring notebook is economical and works best for children (and adults) because they change their minds a lot. It seems to be a source of entertainment, creating a curious sense of satisfaction among children as they sort, arrange, and categorize. The pages can be taken out and rearranged changing a general seasonal journal to specific bird, animal, rocks, and flower sections simply by opening the rings.

Creative disasters lurk around the corner. A glue blob or slip of a felt tip pen can bring a good time to a screeching halt. It is one of the unwritten rules of childhood when disaster occurs on a page to blame a bad pen, wobbly table, a sudden cough etc. and to make the mistake disappear as soon as possible. There is no tearing out pages from a leather bound scrapbook. With the three-ring binder, fresh pages may be added as needed or unsuccessful ones removed by opening the rings.

Arrange a family journal with sections for each family member, should the idea of a journal appeal but seem to overwhelm a young writer. In creating a general family journal, all family members may add to all categories. Add names and dates for future reference. This type of journal is good for someone who is sick in bed or as a conversation piece when a grown child brings home that "special" person for the first time. If you are a person of tradition, you can pass the family journal to an adult child who will continue the tradition.

Journals are useful in the classroom as a cooperative learning project that extends through the school year. Theme possibilities are endless. Some delightful side effects are subtle skill reinforcements in reading (the newspaper, poetry, fiction), in communication (talking to parents, sharing with fellow students), and in listening. The teacher might suggest ideas, but for a successful project, the children must determine the focus of their journals. Topics the teacher could suggest for contemplation are:

Animals (wild or domestic, sightings, pictures, descriptions, original poetry, lines discovered etc.).

Birds (watching, migrating patterns, varieties, favorite foods, nesting habits etc.).

Insects (varieties, function as friend or foe, pictures, drawings, personal encounters, creative writing, news articles).

Heroes (people, pets, news articles, observations, fantasy, poetry etc.).

Recycling (examples of, news articles, personal observations, products developed from recycled materials).

Now you are aware, dear reader, whether you have children, grandchildren, work with children, or feel the child in your soul you can be the quintessential Backyard Naturalist preserving the things special to you.

What To Do
When You Can't Go
Outside

Like trumpets at Jerico, my children's voices sounded early morn-ing news, the news for which all winter weather-watching children wait and mothers dread: "Schools are closed AGAIN today, Mom!"

Never in all my winter parenting days did I have more than an hour between the time of helping the last thumb find the thumb hole in the gloves and locating six pairs of socks to fill up the boots that were too big, before the first child was back for a mitten exchange. Soon my children, each one with a friend or two, were inside searching for something to eat and trying to dry out.

When inclement weather closed the schools for more than one day, and the new snow didn't pack well, an attitude developed. You know the lament – "I'm bored, there's nothing to do." You go down the suggestion list until something appeals to someone, then the others usually join in.

What do you suggest to healthy bouncing children after you've been housebound for several days? It is not like you expected to entertain and shopped for supplies.

Capitalize on this opportunity to break away from television and video games. Please don't think that you must have the blizzard of the century in order to suggest the indoor activities in this section. We all have a rainy Saturday now and then, or a child recovering from illness. Grandparents might have the grandchildren longer than they anticipated. Occasionally, teachers experience that "what now?" feeling as they watch a class consume with lightning speed the lesson plan in half the allotted time. Frequently, the teacher is without that vanishing luxury, the art teacher, and would like to offer simple, "minimal material" projects as motivation, reward or change of pace from the daily routine.

As with all other sections in this book, the ideas are offered as "starters" for your creative thoughts. Maybe some of these ideas are new to you, perhaps others are comfortably familiar. Take the ideas and expand or modify to suit your needs. Flexibility and creative freedom are crucial. Offer an activity suggestion, and back away so the child can develop it.

Once while attending an early childhood education seminar at The College of William and Mary in Williamsburg, Virginia, I sat in on a workshop based on tours and observations of kindergartens in several northern European countries. The leader, drawing interesting parallels through a comprehensive slide presentation and personal observation, discussed activities basic to all kindergarten settings.

One example which interested me was art class in Russia. The children were shown one picture and encouraged to reproduce it in exact detail with identical colors from individual crayon boxes. The room was decorated in an orderly manner with the faithful reproductions hung side by side, evenly spaced.

On the other hand, the children from a kindergarten in Finland were shown a picture and given the suggestion to draw their impressions of what they had just seen. As you may imagine, the results were as varied as the children. Some used the length of the paper, some used the width, and after selecting crayons from the community box in the middle of the table, all used their favorite colors in great abundance.

Times change, governments change, but children are still children. With simple supplies on hand and an out-of-the-way work area where they can slip away and "do their own thing" as creative urges strike, most children find private moments for creative satisfaction.

My daughter Jenny kept her supplies in a shoe box and used the back of an old checkerboard for her work area as she glued strange and wondrous items to her perpetually in-progress project, a collage.

When you were growing up, wasn't there someone in your neighborhood on whom you could rely to supply a missing item to complete a school project – homework predictably left until Sunday evening after all stores were closed?

Although I am a pack rat by nature, I try to put a positive spin on it and call myself frugal. As a result of this frugality, my children and neighbors' children usually were able to root through shoeboxes and shopping bags in the closet to find whatever they needed.

Sometimes storage space is a problem or families move frequently so I have compiled the following list of materials for a "bare bones" all-occasion, never-caught-by-surprise supply box.

The Box

Glue: White craft and paper
Poster board: 1 white piece, 1 colored
Construction paper
Typing paper
Roll of plain (non-adhesive) shelf paper
Paper lace doilies
Scissors
Crayons
Washable felt tip marking pens (fine tip and wide tip)
Jar lid or plastic measuring cup from soft drink mix.
Toothpicks
Glitter and sequins (for older children)
Braid, lace trim, yarn, string
Old magazines with colorful pictures (3 or 4)

Now that the magic box is well-supplied, what about things to do?

Paper Folding

What to do when you can't go outside? You could begin with basic paper folding. Why not recycle some of your newspapers and magazines for general paper folding? Young paper-folding artists are relieved from the pressure of the "just one piece of paper so it has to be perfect the first time" syndrome. The "paper to recycle" supply is bountiful, and the results are often as colorful as they are interesting.

To begin paper folding, please don't say, "Now I'm going to teach you how to fold paper and make fun things," or "Why don't you try paper folding, it's really fun." Get a piece of paper, sit down in a place where you are certain you will be observed, and begin to fold something. So what if you fumble around a little bit, someone will watch you and get curious. The next thing you know, your observer will be a participator.

Guess what! Conversation seems to accompany paper folding. There is something about smoothing those folds that loosens the tongue. Remembering the frustrations my children experienced trying to follow elaborate paper folding project diagrams, I have aimed to keep these projects simple with easy directions. Once basic projects are mastered, check out more sophisticated books from the library. Before long you'll move along with confidence to accept the challenge of Origami, Japanese paper folding.

How To "Square Up" A Piece Of Paper

Many projects require a perfect square of paper. Forget the ruler. There is a very simple way to square up a piece of paper. For practical purposes, assume you will use a standard size piece of notebook paper. Put the paper on a flat surface. If you use your knee as a folding surface, the fold is never as accurate. Take the lower left hand corner and bring it on the diagonal, flush along the top edge to form a perfect triangle. The top left corner becomes a point of the triangle. Notice there is about a 3 inch border on the right. Cut off the excess three inches. Open the paper, and there is the perfect square!

Emergency Paper Cup
MATERIALS:
1 8" X 8" square of clean paper

Directions: Place the square on a flat surface. Fold the square on the diagonal and crease to form a triangle. Visualize for a moment crossing your arms over your chest with right fingertips touching the left shoulder and vice versa. Now turn to the paper. With the center point facing you, take the right point and fold it as you did your arm. The triangle point should come to rest about midway on the opposite side. See the little triangle head appear above the crossed arm? Do the same with the left point.

You will have a double thick triangle peeking above the crossed points. Fold the one triangle tip over the "folded arms." Fold the second triangle tip over the opposite side.

Open up your little cup and enjoy!

Hint: There are many practical as well as fun uses for this cup. Do you have problems taking a pill at a drinking fountain? Do you know a child who can't reach the fountain, or fears the inevitable shot of cold water in the face? How about when no "courtesy cups" are available, or it's flu season, and someone asks for "just a tiny sip." Then there is the unforeseen delay during a class field trip or the long line at the water fountain when three with cups can drink faster than the one "who drinks all the water."

Emergency Baseball Or Football Card Carrier
MATERIALS:
> 1 8" X 11" piece of paper
> Cellophane tape

Directions: Place the paper on a firm surface so that the width is the 11-inch side. Make a 1-inch fold on each border. Next, with the folded borders facing in, fold the paper in half. Fold the rough edges over in a 1-inch fold. Fold the paper in half again so the folded edges face in. Tape two sides leaving the third side open to reveal three pockets that will protect the cards.

Hint: Slip a small piece of cardboard in the center pocket to stabilize the emergency carrier insuring the safety of the card until it makes it home and is slipped into the plastic casing.

The Accordion Fold Fan
MATERIALS:
> Rectangular shape paper: 8" X 11" notebook paper, page from a
magazine etc,
> Clear cellophane tape or stapler
> Crayons or felt tip pens for decorating plain fans

Directions: Place the paper on a firm surface so that the width is the 8-inch side. Hold the top edge of the paper and make a 1-inch fold towards you. Smooth the crease. Hold the folded edge and turn over the paper so that the fold is at the bottom. Still holding the folded edge, turn the edge up away from you folding the paper back on itself in another 1-inch fold.

Repeat this action reversing the folds each time until all the paper is folded. The alternating creases will produce a fan fold. Open and decorate the fan as desired. Close the fan and fold up one end approximately 1 inch to form a small handle.

Tape or staple the handle. Open the fan and use.

Hint: The greater the paper width, the broader the fan. One inch is a nice size fold for less experienced fingers. Whatever size is chosen, the folds should be uniform size for an attractive fan.

Accordion Fold Paper Butterfly
MATERIALS:
1 8" X 8" square of plain paper
1 pipe cleaner
Crayons
1 36" length of string or yarn

Directions: Decorate on all sides both pieces of plain paper. Use accordion fold to crease paper, referring to the directions for an accordion fold fan if necessary. With the "wings" closed at the midway point, pinch the paper tightly, crimping it. Twist the pipe cleaner around the crimp to form the antennae. Tie and knot one end of the yarn around the butterfly middle.

Hint: By eliminating the hanging yarn, the butterfly may be pinned to a curtain or attached to a barrette. Make several sizes and colors of accordion fold butterflies and hang them mobile style from a coat hanger.

Variation: When coloring the butterfly use assorted colors on front and back. Color over all the bright colors with black. With the edge of a penny, a paper clip, toothpick etc., scratch designs in the black crayon. The brilliant colors beneath the black will be revealed.

Accordion Man
MATERIALS:
Scissors
Paper glue, stapler, or cellophane tape

Any type of paper cut in the following sizes:
1 3" X 4" piece for the body
1 2" circle for the head
1 small triangle to fit as a hat
2 1" X 6" strips for the arms
2 1/2" X 1/2" squares for the hands
2 1" X 10" strips for the legs
2 1/2" X 1" rectangles for the feet

Directions: Follow the directions for fan folding, and crease the body in a horizontal or vertical direction. Again using the fan folding directions carefully crease the strips for arms and legs. Glue the hand squares to the ends of the arms. Repeat the process with the feet pieces. Glue the head to the body. Position and glue the arms and legs to the body.

Variation: Design real or imaginary accordion fold animals.

Paper Man With Flexi-Fold Arms And Legs
MATERIALS:
Scissors
Paper glue
Crayons
Protective covering for the work surface such as old plastic place mat or table cloth. Newspaper print might rub off on craft paper.
Construction paper cut into the following shapes:
1 4" X 6" rectangle for body
4 1" X 8" strips for arms
2 1" X 2" ovals for hands
4 1" X 11" strips for legs
2 1" X 2" ovals for feet
1 2" X 2" circle for the head

Directions: Select two strips of paper. Place one in a vertical position and the other in a horizontal position so they form a right angle. Glue the top piece to the bottom and press for a minute to let the glue dry. Paper glue dries much faster than white craft glue. Any excess rubs off the paper.

When folding, visualize the right angle as an "L" and fold the vertical piece toward you. Fold the horizontal piece (the bottom of the "L") to the left. For the next series of folds, bring the vertical strip back up to starting position, and fold the horizontal strip back to the right. An expanding spring-like fold will appear.

Continue alternating folds and directions until both strips are used up. Glue the loose ends and glue on one hand. Proceed in the same manner with the rest of the strips; remember to glue on other hand and both feet. Decorate the face and clothing if you wish. Position the head, arms and legs, then glue them to the body.

Hint: Why not make several friends or by varying sizes create a family? To make a girl use a triangle for the body.

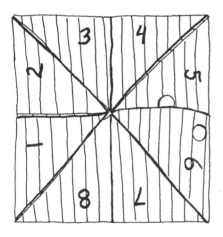 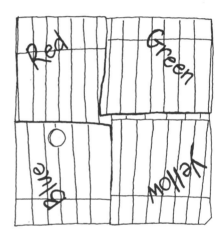

Paper Fortune Teller
MATERIALS:
    1 8" square of plain paper.
    Crayons or felt tip markers

Directions: Place the 8-inch square on a firm surface. Fold each corner point towards the center. All corner points should look like small triangles whose tips meet at the center of the square. When the corner points of the square meet, the paper still resembles a square only smaller. Turn the square over so you don't see the triangles.

Take each tip of the smaller square and again fold towards the center. This will give the effect of having eight smaller triangles. Turn the paper over, and you will see four small squares. Fold the paper in half so the triangles are on the inside. Fold the paper in half again so you have one small square. Undo the last two small folds. Insert thumb and pointer finger under the open ends of the square flaps. The paper figure will open and close like little jaws.

Decoration: Write the names of colors, flowers, animals on the outside squares, with one name to a square. Open the squares to reveal the eight little triangles. Write a number on each little triangle. Lift up the numbered triangle flaps and write fun fortunes such as, "You will receive unexpected wealth, or "You will meet a handsome stranger," etc. on the eight completely concealed spaces. Then refold to finished figure.

To Tell Fortunes: The fortune teller asks the person to select a color and then the moving mini-jaws of the device spells out the color. The device remains open after the last letter to reveal four numbers. The fortune teller then asks the person to select a number. The fortune teller counts out the selected number. There are four numbers exposed after the count. If they are the same, it doesn't matter.

The fortune teller asks the person to select another number, then lifts that number flap and reads the fortune under it.

Easy Six-Fold Sailor's Hat From Newspaper
MATERIALS:
One full size sheet of newspaper

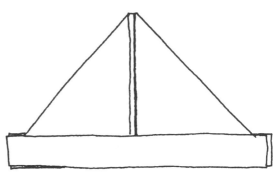

Directions: Fold the paper in half horizontally. With the folded edge away from you and the open side towards you, take the two corners of the folded side and bring them in so they look like triangles and the edges meet along the center of the paper. The triangles will not extend to the open edges of the paper.

Fold one open bottom edge up and over the triangle edge. Repeat the same procedure with the second edge on the other side. Try on the hat.

An Almost Leak Proof Paper Boat
MATERIALS:

1 8" X 11" paper (notebook and inexpensive typing paper work best)

Wax crayon

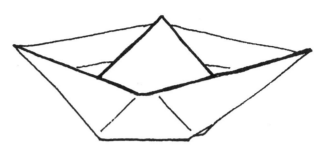

Directions:

Follow the directions for making the Six Fold Sailor's Hat. Open the hat as if to put on. Take the brim points and bring them together to form a square. There will be two little loose flaps on each side. Tuck one flap under the other to make a smooth edge. Next, folding on the horizontal bring first one flap corner then the other up to the opposite corner. You have formed a triangle. (If you look at the opening, it resembles a drinking cup.)

Using both hands, with thumb on the inside of the opening and pointer finger on the outside grasp the triangles at the midway point and open. By bringing the opposite points together a smaller square is formed. Within the new square you will see two triangles. Their tips meet at a third point. Pinch the triangle tips and pull gently in opposite directions – right hand pulls to the right, left hand pulls to the left. You will see a boat emerge.

Using the wax crayon, color the boat on all the exterior surfaces to make it water resistant. Float your boat. Fold a flotilla and have bathtub, sink, or scrub-bucket races.

Newspaper Tree

This is an easy and fun paper project. The unique design stimulates imagination. Those who view the finished product may see a palm tree, a Christmas tree, corn tassel or something befitting King Arthur. The responses are as fun as the creative effort.

MATERIALS:

8 sheets of double wide newspaper

Scissors

Directions: Spread paper out on floor so that it overlaps at least 1/2 of the page. At one end begin to roll the paper. Roll tightly to the end. With scissors cut from the top 2/3rds of the way down. Repeat the cut two more times. Hold the uncut bottom of the newspaper roll in one hand. With the other, reach in the middle, grasp some of the inside strips and pull up.

Repeat the gentle pulling action several times until the tree takes shape. The cut strips become limbs, leaves or whatever the imagination desires.

Hint: For a party decoration spray paint and add glitter, cutouts, string bows etc.

Paper Cutting

Paper cutting may be as simple as cutting one piece of paper in half or as intricate yet delicate as Scherenschnitte designs. As each of my children became interested in using scissors, I started them with a pile of newspapers, especially the colorful Sunday comic sections. As they practiced cutting the rows of funnies apart on the comic page, they learned how to cut straight. They cut in the white spaces between columns. No page was sacred. They cut out editorial cartoons and newspaper photographs. No columnist's picture on the editorial page was spared from the scissors. They branched out to words, and as their cutting dexterity increased they trimmed around individual letters in the headlines.

Eventually one of the children, usually my daughter Jenny, inspired by the multitudinous mound of paper shapes and letters would get out the roll of shelf paper and organize her brothers in a gluing session. Sometimes they worked together, sometimes separately making pictures and collages.

Matt, one of my sons, enjoyed adding glitter, yarn, fabric trims, buttons and anything else that was available to enhance and make his work unique. Chris, the oldest child, enjoyed rummaging through the kitchen cabinets for strangely-shaped objects to use as tracing patterns. Before my youngest child, Sandy, had fingers strong enough to manage scissors, he figured a way to participate in and contribute to the activity. Sandy delighted in ripping paper, sometimes big pieces, sometimes little pieces as his addition to the masterpiece.

When at long last the project under construction was completed and cleaned up, the children would hang their creation on our family room wall and survey it from time to time (until the next creation joined or replaced it) discussing it, pointing to this or that, recalling who spilled juice at what point, how the dog walked on that piece etc.

Paper cutting is fun. The little snippets can be kept under control if cutting is done over a cloth that can be shaken into the trash. Make snowflake or a doll chain to surprise a friend.

A Doll Chain
MATERIALS:

Scissors

1 sheet of typing or construction paper

Very simple pattern (can be made by tracing a gingerbread man cookie cutter)

Directions: Fold the width of the paper in accordion pleats (see accordion fan). The size of the pattern determines the width of the fold. The pattern is to fit with no room to spare. Draw around the pattern. Remove pattern and cut around the tracing line through all the thicknesses of paper. As you cut be very careful to leave a small uncut area by both the right and left hand of the pattern person. This uncut space provides the link that holds the doll chain together. Many children will remember to leave one hand uncut but cut completely around the other and not all the dolls are linked.

Hint: For a very long chain, use a brown grocery bag or shelf paper on a roll. Consider the thickness of the folded paper because scissors will have to cut through all the layers. Sometimes that is a difficult task for children because the fingers are weak, resulting in raggedy edges and exasperated artists.

Sweetheart Chain
MATERIALS:
Scissors
Red construction paper
White construction paper
Paper glue

Directions: Make a heart pattern. Fold and cut the paper as directed for the paper doll chain. Remember to keep the hearts linked, you must leave a small uncut area on the side of each heart curve. When the chain is cut, then cut individual small white hearts and glue on to the large linked hearts.

Linking Rings
MATERIALS:
Construction paper in assorted colors
Scissors
Paper glue

Directions: Cut construction paper in 2- X 8-inch strips (the more strips, the longer the chain). Make a circle from one piece of paper, overlap the ends and glue. Make another circle and link it through the first one. Glue the ends of that circle. Link and glue another circle strip until the chain is the desired length and there are no more paper strips.
Hint: Use those stickers that never made it into sticker albums. Try a little glitter or metallic braid glued to the strips for a decorative touch.

Flying Fish
MATERIALS:
Construction paper cut in a 3" X 11" strip
Scissors
Yarn
Felt tip marking pens or crayons
Directions: Decorate both sides of the strip if desired. Fold the

strip in half. Hold the strip with the fold in your left hand and prepare to make a cut about 1 1/2-inch from the bottom of the top end. Cut in only about 3/4-inch.

Turn the strip over still holding the fold in your left hand. Again cut in about 3/4-inch on the strip which is now on top. Fit the cuts together and where the cuts intersect, the fish tail is formed. Decide where on the back you wish to fasten the yarn hanger. Poke a hole through the back.

Thread the yarn through the hole and tie a knot. With clear cellophane tape secure the knot under the back so it won't pull through the hole.

Snowflakes

The beauty of this paper cutting project is that just as all real snowflakes are different so are the cut ones. The possibilities are limitless with each fold and snip.

MATERIALS:
1 4" X 4" piece of white paper
1 sheet of colored construction paper
Paper glue
Scissors
Drop cloth (to collect the cuttings, to provide a speedy cleanup)

Directions: Fold the square in half. Fold it in half again. Fold to form a triangle. Hold the folded tip of the triangle in one hand and cut off the bottom third of the triangle. Cut a small part off the folded tip. Cut out "V" notches on the folds. Open the snowflake.

If you want more design, refold and cut more notches. If you want larger snowflakes, begin with larger squares. Reduce the size of the square for smaller flakes. To vary the edges, cut notches there too.

For a variety of shapes, change the way you fold and also angle the cut of the edge. Use quick drying paper glue to mount the white snowflake on colored paper.

Hint: Create a snowstorm by cutting snowflakes of various sizes and shapes. Tape them to windows, mirrors or a large glass door. Why not use thread and extend the snowflakes from an overhead ceiling light?

Pinwheel
MATERIALS:
1 square of colored paper
Straight pin
Unsharpened pencil with good eraser or plastic drinking straw
Scissors
A dime
Sharpened pencil, pen or felt tip marker

Directions: Fold the paper on the diagonal to form a triangle. Open the paper and fold on the diagonal the opposite way. When you open the paper you will see four triangles. Place the dime where the folds intersect in the center of the paper, and draw a circle around the dime. Very carefully cut on the fold lines, towards the center. Do not cross the line and cut into the little circle.

Now the square is cut, and there are eight points.

Bring points one, three, five, and seven to the circle. Stick the pin through them and then into the pencil eraser. Blow the pinwheel and watch it spin. If the pinwheel doesn't spin very well, check the pin to see that it is not pressing the points too tightly into the eraser.

Hint: For a kaleidoscopic effect use white paper as the base and color each triangular fold a different color.

Three Dimensional Paper Flowers
MATERIALS:
Double thickness facial tissue
Thread
Pipe cleaner

Directions: Fold the tissue in half lengthwise. Using the accordion fold, crease the tissue in 1/2-inch folds. Pinch the middle of the accordion folded tissue and tie a piece of string securely around the pinched middle. Trim the folds from one end. (The other end is open.)

Loop and twist the pipe cleaner around the tied center, securing and twisting the end of the pipe cleaner underneath the tissue. To finish the flower gently pull the layers of tissue apart and fluff them.

Hint: Create a colorful paper flower by using four layers of assorted colors of tissue. (Not facial, but tissue used as wrapping paper.)

Paper Flower With Curled Petals

MATERIALS:

Assorted colors of construction paper
4 circular patterns (jar lid, drinking glass, juice glass, and nickel)
Scissors
Round toothpick
Paper glue

Directions: Select the colored paper for the flower. Trace around the circles and cut out all but the smallest circle. Use a different color for the smallest circle which will be the center of the flower. Put a dot of paper glue in the center of the large and medium circles and glue them together, placing the small circle on the medium, and the medium on the large.

Carefully cut into the circles to make a fringe look. Try to space the cuts as evenly as possible without cutting clear to the center point. After the entire circle is fringed, cut out and glue the smallest (nickel) circle to the center. Roll several fringe petals around a round toothpick. (For less dexterous younger children, instead of a toothpick I choose a crochet hook. I favor a crochet hook over a knitting needle because it is shorter and has a blunt end.)

Work your way around the flower rolling the fringe until all the petals are curled. Choose a leaf pattern and cut two or three leaves from green construction paper. Glue the leaves to the back of the flower.

Hint: A smaller flower may be used to decorate notepaper. Several flowers can be glued to a strip of felt or burlap ribbon to make a wall hanging. Create a picture, decorate a bedroom mirror, or make a mobile.

Ornamental Paper Lantern

The size of this lantern can be altered to suit the need or the season. Very tiny lanterns can be made for Christmas and Easter trees, larger ones for birthday or other celebrations. Remember the potential fire hazard of paper so do not put candles, lightbulbs or other heat-producers in these paper lanterns!

MATERIALS:

Wallpaper scraps, construction paper
Tissue paper
Scissors
Paper glue

Directions: Cut a 1- X 4-inch strip of paper for the handle. Cut a 6- X 10-inch strip of paper. Fold it in half length wise. Make a series of cuts at 1-inch intervals on the fold. Each cut should stop 1/2-inch from the raw edge of the paper. Unfold the paper and curve it into a circle to see the lantern shape. If the cuts are even, glue the raw edges.

Tuck the handle edges in the upper rim of the lantern and glue in place.

Hint: For a "glowing" lantern," before gluing the lantern edges, open the paper and glue colored tissue paper to the inside of the lantern. Trim off any excess tissue paper, then glue the lantern edges together.

Paper Air Balls

This is a no-mess, no-fail project for small people or the convalescent child who is getting better, but is still short on patience and lasting energy.

MATERIALS:

Gummed stars or other stickers
Colored paper
Yarn
Scissors
Paper glue

Directions: Cut three 1-X 8-inch strips of colored paper. Decorate the strips with stars or stickers. Bend one decorated strip into a circle, overlap the ends slightly and glue the ends together. Repeat the process with two more decorated strips. Carefully fit the circles together so they form a ball. At the point the circles intersect at top and bottom, glue them together.

Make a loop hanger from the yarn and glue it to the top of the ball. Hang the ball somewhere so light will catch the shiny stars, and air current will gently turn it.

Paper Spirals

This paper figure makes a good contrasting companion for the Paper Air Ball.

MATERIALS:

Brown grocery bag or heavy construction paper (the larger the paper, the larger the spiral)
Pan lid, pie pan, mixing bowl etc. for circular pattern
Scissors

    Paper glue
    Glitter or very light-weight metallic braid
    Yarn or string

Directions: If making a large spiral from a grocery bag, cut open the bag and remove the bottom. Press the brown paper with a warm iron to remove wrinkles, fold lines etc. Position the pattern and cut the largest circle the paper will allow. Make a cut in the paper and cut about 1 inch from the edge until you have gone all the way around the circle.

Keep cutting, spiraling inward turning the paper as you cut until you have reached the center. Following the spiral pattern, decorate top and bottom. Make a loop from string and glue it to the center of the spiral. When the glue is dry, lift the spiral up by the string loop so it opens and extends. Hang from a curtain rod, light fixture etc.

Mini Paper Basket

Start small with this basket. It is ideal for a special gift. Increase the dimensions for a larger basket.

MATERIALS:
    Construction paper
    Scissors
    Ruler
    Paper glue
    Crayons, rick rack, stickers, glitter or other trim.

Directions: Cut a 5- X 5-inch square of paper. Cut a 1- X 6-inch strip of paper. Beginning at the top left edge of the square, measure and mark at 1 1/2 inches. Continue along the edge and make a mark at the 3 1/2-inch point. Do the same measurement for the bottom edge. These measurements are the cut marks. On each of the dots, measure and draw a straight line 1 1/2-inches towards the center. This is the cut line.

Measure and draw straight lines from the other three dots and cut as you did with the first one.

To Form The Basket: Fold the end pieces towards the center. Make a smooth crease then open the flaps. Fold the uncut center flaps towards the middle, crease and open. Bring the end flaps around so they meet. Bring the large center piece up and glue the end flaps to the center piece. Repeat on the other end.

When the flaps are glued in place, the corners form a smooth crisp fold. Glue the handle ends on the inside of the basket where the end flaps join.

Paper Dolls

These beauties are in a class by themselves. During World War II when I was four and five, I had several serious bouts with pneumonia. While I had to spend so much time in bed, my Aunt Janey who lived far away designed a paper doll which as I look at her today (yes, I still have the doll and paper clothes) suspiciously resembled the 4-year-old me. It was an event to receive letters addressed to me because I knew a pretty little dress would flutter out of the envelope for dolly. The paper was WWII texture and coloring was done with colored pencils, but I had a wonderful time.

The summer I was nine I spent on the front porch recovering from a severe, blistering sunburn. Paper dolls were again my ticket away from boredom.

Directions: Draw, color and cut out a paper doll from plain paper. Mount the doll on posterboard and trim away excess. For durability in small hands consider covering the doll with clear self adhesive paper. Make more clothing by tracing around the doll, cutting out and coloring the items. Decorate a shoebox or flip top box to keep the doll and clothes from harm's way.

Variation: Cut complete figures from clothing catalogs. Cut clothing making sure to cut generous "fold over" tabs.

Paper Weaving

Although paper weaving takes a little patience, the end result is instantly recognizable, colorful and in most cases useful. Let the shape, size and imagination dictate the use. The small squares make nice "mug" mats or coasters. The larger rectangular pieces work well as placemats, plant mats to protect tables, bedside table or dresser "scarves." Rule of thumb: Small fingers are more successful with larger materials.

Woven Placemat
MATERIALS:

2 pieces of 9" X 12" colored construction paper
Ruler

Pencil
Scissors
Paper glue

Directions: First determine the width of the borders. The directions for this mat is for one-inch borders.

On the "wrong side" of the paper with the ruler at the top, measure down 1 inch and mark with a dot in three spots. Repeat this process along the bottom, measuring up and marking 1 inch in three spots. Hold the ruler to connect the dots and lightly draw lines to identify the border so it won't accidentally be cut.

Make dots along the width of the paper at 1/2-inch intervals. Repeat at the opposite end. Lay the ruler from dot to corresponding dot the length of the paper and lightly draw cutting lines. By using 9-inch wide paper, you should have 15 cutting lines. Cut on the lines. Adults may prefer cutting on an indestructible surface with single edge craft razor. A craft razor in the hand of well-supervised children can still mar a table top or slice a knuckle. For children using scissors there is less opportunity for an untimely mishap.

Carefully fold the paper in half; on the folded width make small cuts on each line. Open the paper, stick one end of the scissors through the hole and cut the length of the line to the margin on the left side. Return to center and cut to the margin on the other end.

Repeat the cutting process until all 15 lines are cut. Cut 20 1/2-inch strips of contrasting colored construction paper.

Weaving: Begin the weaving at one end, not in the center. It is too hard adjusting the strips. On the "wrong" or "under" side of the mat feed a strip of colored paper through the slit to the "up" side. Weave over the first bar, under the second etc. finishing with the raw end on the underside.

Take another strip and weave the opposite way, under then over, finishing again with the raw end on the underside. After each strip is woven, press gently against that strip, easing it toward the other strips, eliminating any gaps.

Repeat the alternating "over/under" or "under/over" weaving until all the strips are used. Glue the raw ends on the underside of the mat.

Woven Heart
MATERIALS:
1 sheet 9" X 12" red construction paper

1 sheet white paper (typing or construction)
Heart pattern cut from scrap paper
Pencil
Scissors
Paper glue

Directions: Fold red paper lengthwise. Fold heart pattern in half and lay the heart fold on the paper fold. Trace pattern and cut heart from red paper. Read woven placemat general directions for measuring and cutting. Keeping the 1-inch borders, measure the length of the heart from between the mounds to the tip point of the heart. Now space the cut lines at 1-inch intervals to the right and to the left of the center line. Cut as directed.

Prepare 1-inch wide white strips for weaving and proceed as directed for weaving the placemat. Trim ends of strips if necessary and glue the ends on the under side of the heart.

Hint: Make small woven hearts and glue to folded paper to make greeting cards. Do not limit yourself or children to traditional red and white. Although hearts are traditionally associated with Valentine's day, they offer myriad possibilities such as personalizing correspondence or thank you notes, and birthday or get-well messages.

Brown Grocery Bag Reversible Woven Placemat
MATERIALS:

2 full size brown grocery bags to make one 12" x 15" placemat
Pencil
Ruler
Scissors
Iron
White craft glue
Stapler

Directions: Cut down the side of the paper bag and remove the bottom. With a cool iron press the wrinkles and creases out of the brown paper. Measure and cut 30 4- X 15-inch strips. Fold each strip in half lengthwise and iron the seam. Open each strip. Again lengthwise, bring the raw edge on the right into the center fold and press.

Do the same with the raw edge on the left of the center fold. With the raw edges folded in toward the center, now refold the center to make a study 1-inch strip. Repeat this with the other strips.

Weaving Directions: Set aside four strips for the borders. Strip one is the anchor strip. Lay one end of strip number two on top of the end of strip number one to form a right angle. Position strip three with its end under the anchor strip but right next to strip number two. Alternate over/under, over/under until 14 strips are stapled to the anchor strip. (At this point it may look like a giant floppy comb!)

Assuming you will work left to right, strip number two (remember strip one is the anchor across the top.) becomes the anchor strip on the side. Select a strip and staple it on top of strip two side by side next to strip number one. Begin the under/over weaving. With each strip you will weave the opposite of the preceding one. If you began over/under with strip three, then begin under/over with strip four. Do this until all the strips are stapled and woven.

After the mat is woven, adjust the strips so there are no gaps; staple the unstapled ends. To complete the finished edges around the mat, glue one folded strip across the top and one folded strip across the bottom, making sure the raw edge of the mat fits into the fold for a nice finish on both sides of the mat.

On both ends of the remaining finishing strips, fold the corners in to the center fold, giving an arrow-like point, and press the folds. Glue these strips over the remaining raw edges. Use a book or other heavy object to press the finished edges until the white craft glue dries.

Strings And Things

Who can imagine life without string or a ball of yarn? Neither do I knit nor do I crochet, but I seem to have bags of yarn. I did put in my time with the knitting needles and crochet hooks making long shapeless, nameless strips as my grandmother, aunts and mother clicked knitting needles at breakneck pace creating sweaters and the multi-yarn, multi-needle argyle socks.

Eventually, I found my own satisfying uses for string and yarn. Anyone with a knitting or crocheting auntie or grandmother should remember holding out both arms while auntie was "balling the yarn." As a child, not knowing the practicality of it, I believed "balling the yarn" was an activity designed for my pleasure.

As I began to work with yarn, I thought I could use the skein as it came from the store. Wrong. Soon I had a knotted mess, lost lengths of yarn, and realized how important it was to "ball the yarn" before using it. If willing arms are not available or get tired, slip the loop of yarn around the back of a chair and roll the yarn into a ball.

On rainy Saturday mornings my younger children made string trails, string mazes and at least twice during the winter Jenny, Matt and Sandy looped yarn around the bathroom, various bedroom door knobs and down the hall. The "trap" was designed to "challenge" their sleeping big brother Chris as he bolted from bed and flung wide his bedroom door, emerging to answer the telephone call they claimed was for him.

String painting emerged near the top of the list as a favorite rainy day activity for two reasons. We never had enough little paintbrushes to go around, and string painting reduced the inevitable frustration that came when the brush picture didn't turn out to the artist's satisfaction.

Although water-base latex, tempera and other paints work well and generally last "for the life of the paper," I preferred to use a non-toxic, easy to cleanup homemade paint for the younger children because the string painting usually took a turn for the messy and became a finger painting session. Most important, I always had the ingredients on hand!

Homemade Paint For String Painting
MATERIALS:
> 1/4 Cup all purpose flour
> 1 1/4 cups water
> Red, green or blue food coloring
> Saucepan (1-quart size)
> Spoon

Directions: Measure flour into saucepan. Add 1/2 cup of water to the flour and stir until the flour and water mixture is smooth. Stir in the rest of the water.

Place saucepan over medium heat and heat slowly, stirring constantly. As it heats, the mixture will thicken and begin to shine.

When the paint reaches the desired consistency remove from the heat. (You don't want GLOBS of paint; desired consistency is what ever degree of thickness you think will work best. Add more water if the paint gets too thick, and add flour it you want a thicker paint for fingerpainting.)

Mix in the food coloring of choice until the paint reaches the desired color.

String Painting With Homemade Paint
MATERIALS:

> 18 inches of string or yarn
> White shelf paper, construction paper, typing paper
> Foil pie pan
> Newspaper or washable covering for the work surface

Directions: Place string or yarn in pie pan so it will soak up the paint. When the string or yarn has become thoroughly saturated, grasp both ends of the string, carefully pick it up, and arrange it on the paper.

At this point some artists may consider the work complete. If so, carefully lift the string from the paper. Others may wish more intricate designs. To continue, lift the string, and if it needs more paint, return it to the paint pan. If not, arrange the string on the paper in a complementary pattern with the first print.

Copycat String Painting
MATERIALS:

> 12 inches of string or yarn
> White or solid color construction paper
> Paint
> Foil pie pan
> Newspaper or other washable covering for work surface

Directions: Cover work surface. Place paint in pie pan. Saturate string or yarn in paint. Fold paper in half (either width or length) and open.

Arrange string on 1/2 of the paper. Refold the paper and press down with gentle pats on the area above the string or yarn. Open the folded paper and carefully remove the string or yarn.

Hint: Slight movement of the string or yarn while it is beneath the folded paper produces an interesting variation.

String Picture
MATERIALS:

> Construction paper
> String or yarn
> White craft glue
> Jar lid or small plastic measuring cup from powdered drink mix
> Scissors

Newspaper or washable covering for work surface
Wet sponge in a dish for sticky fingers

Directions: Put glue in jar lid. Cut lengths of string or yarn and one at a time saturate the pieces with glue. Lift each piece of string or yarn out of the glue and arrange on the paper to dry in place. Add as many colors and textures of string and yarn as you wish in free form or geometric shapes.

The glue will be clear when the picture is dry.

Variation: Cut shapes from fabric or wallpaper scraps and glue them to the construction paper. Glue the string or yarn around the edges of the shapes.

String and Nail Free Form Art
MATERIALS:
1 6" X 6" square of plywood
Finishing nails
Hammer
Colored thread, string, yarn etc.

Directions: All the way around the square, hammer the nails 1 inch from the edge of the plywood. Securely wrap the string three times around the bottom left corner nail. Criss-cross the string in any pattern or direction between nails, wrapping once around each nail and tying securely around the final nail when the design is completed.

If the artist does not wish this to be a permanent creation he/she may unwind the thread and create again and again.

Vase Decorated With String
MATERIALS:
Juice can, glass bottle, aluminum can or any round-sided container
Coarse rug yarn (the quantity depends on the size of the container to be covered)
Felt or cardboard
Scissors
White craft glue
Paper cup or a small, reusable plastic measuring cup found in powdered drink mix containers
Small paint brush or flat wooden craft stick
Newspaper or washable cover for the work surface
Wet sponge in a dish for wiping fingers

Directions: Cut one 24-inch length of any color yarn. Unless you are using a very small container, you will need to cut more yarn when this piece is glued down. Don't try to work with yarn long enough to cover the entire can because it will get tangled. If you leave the length of yarn attached to the ball, the ball usually gets away, unrolls and is a snarly mess. When it comes time to cut the second length of yarn, you may use the same color or change colors for a variegated design.

Put a couple of tablespoons of glue in the glue cup. Start at the base of the can and spread a strip of glue approximately 1 inch around the can. Pressing the end of the yarn into the glue with your thumb, coil the yarn around the can until the glued surface is covered with yarn. (It might be easier at first to turn the can upside down until the yarn half covers the can.)

Spread more glue and repeat coiling until the entire length of yarn is used. Cut another length of yarn (the same color or different). Angle the new yarn so that the end begins about a half an inch before the old strip ends and press it into the glue with your thumb.

On the second coil around the can wrap over the new end and continue in this manner until the entire can is covered.

Gold braid, yarn bows, buttons etc. may be added after the yarn is dry. Trace the bottom of the can on cardboard or felt. Cut out the circle and glue to the bottom of yarn covered can. The vase is complete!

Hint: A gluing option is to dip the yarn in glue and wrap the can. This works but can get very messy. If the artist is not a speedy worker, yarn and fingers get very sticky.

Gift Ideas: Small juice cans can certainly be used as pencil holders, containers for office supplies, on dressers as holders for barrettes and pony tail elastics, or in the kitchen to collect small change or lunch money.

Variation: Collect thin, young honeysuckle, kudzu or other wild, nuisance, non-poisonous vines to glue and coil around 16 ounce or larger cans. Glue vines to cans the same way as the yarn. Patience is necessary as the vines must be held in place as the glue dries.

The Eye Of God (Multi-Colored Four-Point Yarn Star)
MATERIALS:

2 6" sticks
Rug yarn scraps in assorted lengths and colors

Directions: Tie the sticks together at right angles to form a cross. With one hand hold an end of the yarn under the wooden cross where the sticks intersect. Beginning with the right hand stick and weaving in a counter-clockwise direction, bring the yarn around the top of the right-hand stick, under it in a looping fashion, then up and over and looping around the next up-right stick. Work around all the prongs of the star as many times as you want until the yarn runs out or you want to change colors.

To change colors finish looping on the underside. Cut off the extra yarn if necessary, but be sure to leave a 3- to 4-inch tail. Loop the tail around once and tuck it up under the loop. Pull tightly to secure in a "self-knot."

Tie on the new yarn to the tail or double knot tightly around the stick. Weave according to the directions. To finish the project, knot the yarn around the stick and trim the tails. To decorate the tips glue on yarn streamers or pompoms.

Variation: Use double tip cotton swabs for small stars.

Yarn Decorated Box
MATERIALS:
Small, square, white cardboard gift box
Coarse rug yarn
White craft glue
Jar lid
Scissors
Toothpick
Wet sponge in a dish for wiping hands

Directions: Before removing the top of the box, make a mark on the bottom portion at the edge of the lid. Measure the perimeter of the bottom portion of box, add 1/2-inch and cut the appropriate length of yarn.

Cut five additional lengths of yarn. More can be cut if needed, however the yarn must not extend into the area covered by the lid, otherwise the lid will not fit properly.

Spread white glue on one side of the box. Take six lengths of yarn, arrange these lengths of yarn in close rows leaving about one-half inch yarn tails extending beyond the box. For best results set the box aside for about an hour while the glue sets up on the first side. This wait is not necessary for the three remaining sides.

Apply glue to the adjoining side and bring the yarn around to the second side. If you have not let the glue dry on the first side, be careful not to pull the yarn as you bring it around the corner. Apply glue to the third side and fourth sides, arranging the yarn as directed.

If the yarn rows do not reach the box top mark, cut enough strands to fill the gap and glue as directed. Set the box aside to dry. To decorate the top, measure and cut enough strands of yarn to cover the sides and follow instructions for gluing the bottom of the box.

Suggestions for decorating the top of the box:

Using a toothpick make a glue outline of a word such as "Mom," "thread," "coins," "keys" etc. Or using a toothpick make a simple outline of a flower, bird, car etc. and arrange yarn on top of the glue to create the design.

Yarn Coasters
MATERIALS:
   Rug yarn
   Plastic lids from margarine tubs, soft drink mix cans etc.
   White craft glue
   Wooden craft stick for spreading glue
   Scissors
   Newspapers or other protective covering for work surface
   Wet sponge in a dish for wiping hands

Directions: With the wooden craft stick, smooth a thick layer of glue around the inside of the plastic lid.

It is not necessary to precut the yarn before gluing it. Begin at the edge and circle the yarn around until it is coiled to the center. Cut the yarn and tuck the end under the final coil. Let the coaster dry.

To finish the coaster, measure, cut and glue a length of yarn around the outer edge of the lid.

Yarn Doll #1
MATERIALS:
   Yarn
   Scissors
   1 3" X 5" index card

Directions: Wrap the yarn 20 times around the 5-inch sides of the index card. Cut the yarn from the ball. Holding the yarn covered card in one hand, cut the wrapped yarn across the bottom of the card. The doll's head is the uncut end, so measure down 1 inch and tie off the head with a piece of yarn.

Count out 10 strands for one arm, tie off with yarn and cut the ends to make them shorter than the body strands. Count 10 strands for the other arm, tie off with yarn and cut to match the first arm.

Tie a piece of yarn around the middle of the body to shape the waist. Divide the following strands to make the legs and tie off each leg at the "ankle" to form the feet.

Hint: To make a girl doll, tie the waist with ribbon sash and do not tie up the legs. Trim the strands for an even edge on the skirt.

Yarn Doll #2
MATERIALS:
Yarn
Scissors
1 4" X 6" cardboard

Directions: Wrap the yarn 20 times around 6-inch side of the card. Cut the yarn at one end. On the uncut end measure down about an inch and tie off the head. To create lengths of yarn for the arms wrap the yarn 10 times around the 4-inch side. Slip the yarn off the card. Cut the loops on one end and tie. Repeat the cut and tie procedure on the other end.

Slip this little bundle sideways through the body strands to form arms. Tie a piece of yarn around the doll to form the waist just below the arms. Divide the strands into two bunches of 10 and tie off with yarn for the legs. Trim any uneven ends on the hands and feet.

Hint: Turn this into a holiday doll by using white yarn and lace for an angel, red and white yarn for a Santa, or black and orange colors for a Halloween doll.

Fluffy Yarn Ball
MATERIALS:
1 36" length of any color yarn or three 12" lengths of assorted colors
1 6" length of yarn
Scissors
1 3" width of cardboard

Directions: Wrap the length of yarn around the 3-inch cardboard as many times as it will go. Slide the yarn off the cardboard and securely tie the 6-inch length of yarn around the center of the wrapped yarn. Cut the loops on both ends and fluff the yarn.

Hint: Make various sizes of fluffy poms, tie them together and create an interesting yarn menagerie. Make poms in school or seasonal colors. Glue colorful pom to barrette or tie pom into shoelace bow.

Making Toys

Most of these games and toy suggestions are familiar favorites beloved by my children and simple to create. Hopefully, the assortment will bring to mind happy days and toys of your childhood. This starter assortment is to get you underway. Let creativity and imagination take hold and see what curious and wonderful ideas emerge.

Bubble Blowing
BUBBLE SOLUTION MATERIALS:

1/2 cup dishwashing liquid

1 cup lukewarm water

1 teaspoon glycerin (optional, will give longer lasting bubbles)

Plastic margarine tub

Spoon

Directions: Pour dishwashing liquid into plastic tub. Stirring very slowly and gently to prevent foaming, pour 1/2 cup water into the dishwashing liquid. Add the glycerin and the remaining water and again stir very gently.

BUBBLE BLOWING DEVICE MATERIALS:

A plastic drinking straw

A slotted spoon, spatula with slots or other curious shapes from the kitchen

An empty spool

Flexible wire or large paper clips twisted into circles of various sizes. Pipe cleaners can be used in emergencies but get very soggy and drippy.

Directions: For cascading bubbles: pour a small amount of bubble solution in a custard cup size container, place a plastic drinking straw in the solution, and blow into the solution. Bubbles will form and cascade over the side. (Blow only! A mouthful of bubble soap is really yucky.) For floaters, dip the blowing device such as a slotted spoon or slotted spatula in the bubble solution and wave it through the air. To use a spool, dip one end of the spool into the solution and blow through the other end. When using wire rings simply dip in and blow through the ring or twirl around and watch the bubbles float.

Spinning Top
MATERIALS:
Leftover sharpened pencil stubs (or nail about 4" long)
Electrical tape
Poster board or other heavy cardboard
Lid from 18-ounce peanut butter jar, lid from 1-pound coffee can or other circular pattern.
Scissors

Directions: Wrap tape in spirals around pencil or nail from top to bottom, including the tip, to create the spindle. Trace around the pattern to make a circle on the cardboard. Cut out the circle and decorate with felt marking pens, stickers etc. Make a hole in the center of the circle.

Cover the hole on the underside with tape and reopen the hole through the tape. This will reinforce the hole and make the top last longer. Spin the top.

Hint: Have "spin offs" with the tops. The longest spinning, the one that can spin without falling off the table or leaving a designated area are some activities. The length of spinning time can be controlled by how far up or down the spindle the cardboard ring is.

Insert the pencil through the center hole and adjust the cardboard ring.

Variation: Mentally divide the circle into fourths. In each fourth about midway between the pencil and the edge of the paper cut a 1-inch flexible air flap in the circle. Fold the flaps up or down and experiment with spinning.

Button Spinner
MATERIALS:

> Large, heavy coat button with two holes
> 1 36" length of string
> 1 1" plastic cafe curtain rings (optional)

Directions: Thread the string through one button hole. Thread the string back through the other hole. Slide the button to the center of the string and tie the ends of the string securely together. Either tie finger hole knots on each end or use a slip knot to attach a curtain ring at each end of the string.

Directions for working the spinner: Stick your forefinger in the loop on each end or hold a ring in each hand and twirl string and the button several times until the string is twisted on either side of the button. Quickly, in a pulling motion, move the hands out. This action will make the string taut as the button spins. Move both hands in and pull out again.

Repeat this action over and over, faster and faster.

Hint: To make a slip knot for the rings, bring the loop of string through the plastic ring. Spread the loop and pull the rest of the string, including the button, through the loop and pull to secure the knot.

Whizzer
MATERIALS:

> 1 12" ruler or stick of similar length
> 1 36" length of strong twine
> Corrugated cardboard
> Scissors
> Masking tape

Directions: Cut a diamond shape approximately eight inches long and three inches wide. Poke a hole approximately 1 inch up from the tip on the length. Reinforce the hole with masking tape. Tie one end of the string securely through the hole and tie the other string around the yardstick at about the 9-inch mark. If the yardstick has a hanging hole, run the string through that and tie it securely.

How to use: Take the whizzer outside where there is plenty of room. Grasp the stick with one hand or both and in a circular motion swing the tethered diamond high above the head. Increase momentum and the sound increases. A more sophisticated swing is accomplished by using one hand or two method to grasp the stick. Hold the stick in front of you and swing in a figure-8 motion, over and over again. To increase momentum is to increase the noise.

Hint: If everyone enjoys this toy, make a more durable one from a lightweight material such as balsa wood.

Ring And Cup

A favorite of whittlers and wood workers, this toy can be crafted from all types of soft wood, sanded and finished. Many variations of this game exist. Some call for a ring, others for a wooden ball. The challenge is the same: catch the object in the cup.

Not all of us are woodcrafters, nor do we have access to woodworking tools. Should you wish to pursue wooden toy making, plan to have your first stop at the local library to determine the investment you must make in time, space, materials and machinery.

This version is a do-it-now toy and the following materials list is composed of items usually found about the house. These directions call for such common items.

MATERIALS:

Small plastic ring (no larger than 1-inch in diameter)
Small plastic cup used to measure powdered soft drink mix
Straight stick, or wooden dowel (10" or 12" length)
String (26" to 30" length)
Scissors
White craft glue

Directions To Make: Trim the handle off the little plastic cup. Glue the cup to the stick about 1 inch from the end of the stick and set aside for about 2 hours to let the glue dry.

Tie the plastic ring to one end of the string. Check to see if the cup is firmly glued to the stick, then tie the other end of the string around the end of the stick.

Directions To Play: Hold the stick in one hand. Move the stick back and forth, all around so the ring and string swing through the air.

The object is through eye/hand coordination to try to catch the flying ring in the cup without your other hand touching it. Go ahead, you know you want to play. Set a timer and see how many catches you can make before the 1-minute or 5-minute ding.

Hint: If a ring is not available, use a small cork or a small plastic pill bottle lid. Knot the string and with a straight pin, attach it to the cork. Poke a hole in the little lid.

Variation: Simplify things, and tie one end of a length of string around a stick and the other end of the string around a ring from a canning jar or a large wooden drapery ring. Catch the ring on the stick.

Flip Flap

This toy, also called Jacob's Ladder, is easy to construct and amazing to watch in motion. Does it move in ripples or is it an optical illusion? This seemingly unanswerable question is forever open to discussion.

MATERIALS:

6 2" X 2" squares cut from 1/2" plywood
Sandpaper
Wood stain and staining cloth (optional)
Narrow ribbon or flat cotton tape (preferably 1/4" width but no wider than 1/2")
Scissors
White craft glue
Newspapers

Directions: Cover the work surface with newspaper. Sand the squares until no rough edges remain. Select three of the squares and stain a dark brown according to the directions on the can of stain if you wish to have a colorful flip flap.

When the staining is finished, place the squares of wood in a line on the table. Put a drop of glue at the center of the top edge on the first block and without cutting the tape, put the end of the tape in the glue. Run tape behind the first square and guide the tape down the front of the second square, then behind the third, in front of the fourth etc. until the tape is woven through all the squares. Glue the tape at the center top edge of each square.

After the tape is down the final side, pull it gently so it is taut and allow for about one quarter overlap. Cut and glue the tape at the center bottom edge. Two more tapes will be threaded on either side of the center tape through the squares in similar fashion. It is easier to thread both tapes before gluing.

Glue the tapes to the bottom edge of the first square. Keep in mind, when the center tape is in back, the two tapes are threaded to run down the front. Alternate showing the single and double tapes until reaching the bottom of the last square. The double tapes should be pulled taut and glued at the bottom of each square.

Let the glue dry completely before playing with the Flip Flap.

Directions For Playing With The Flip Flap: Hold the top square in your hand and tip it back and forth. The other blocks flip flap down in a constant tumbling motion.

Hint: For immediate use, assemble the Flip Flap with small staples instead of glue.

Stilts

Is there a bit of circus performer in all of us? Is that why stilts appeal? A few inches off the ground do we see things from a different perspective? Maybe the precursor to stilts, perhaps the sign of readiness for stilts at my house came as each of my children in turn grew tired of holding on to my hands, positioning their feet on top of mine, moving as I moved with big steps, little steps, side steps.

Can-Man Stilts
MATERIALS:

2 clean 16-ounce aluminum cans or 1-pound coffee cans with one end still in

Clothesline
Awl

Directions: Turn the can upside down so that the closed end becomes the top. With the awl punch two holes about an inch from the top on opposite sides of the can. Repeat the hole punching making two holes in the other can.

Without cutting, thread the clothesline in one hole and out through the other, pulling a considerable length through. Have the stilt walker stand on the threaded can (have the unthreaded can nearby for the other foot) and bring up the clothesline to a satisfactory handle length. Cut and tie. Repeat this with the other stilt can.

Directions for Walking on Can-Man Stilts: Stand on the cans and hold on to the clothesline handles, and lift the can up with each foot as you walk.

Big Man Stilts

Not too long ago many kids were able to go out back, up the hill, or hike over to a wooded lot to find young trees suitable for stilt making. The major requirement was a young tree with a sturdy branch growing out in a "V" form. Next job was to strip away excess leaves and branches, and finally, break off the special branch to form a "V" which would serve as the foot rest for the stilt. Spare the trees that are still growing! These days the building supply store is the place to get materials for stilts. As a rule someone is available to cut wood to specification so go prepared with measurements.

These stilts require some assembly time and tools.

MATERIALS:

1 board, 2" x 4" measuring 6 feet long, cut into two 2" X 2" X 5' lengths

2 right angle wood triangles cut from the remaining one foot length

Sandpaper

Hammer and nails

Stain or paint (Optional)

Directions: Sand the long strips until smooth. Measure and mark one foot up from the end of each pole for the foot rests. Placing the long side of the triangle against the pole, hammer the nail in part way near the bottom until certain of positioning. It is at this point you can change the position of the foot support by removing the nail. When satisfied, complete the nailing and adding three additional nails. Paint if desired.

Directions For Using Tall Man Stilts: Inexperienced stilt walkers may require an adult to stabilize the poles as the walker steps onto the foot supports. Some prefer to stand on a chair and step down while others remain on the floor and step up. Although walking is not difficult, the tricky part seems to be getting balanced on the second stilt.

Repeat the procedure with the second pole and triangle.

Kitchen Creativity

Remember when the kitchen was filled with wondrous aromas of muffins, biscuits, cookies or loaves of freshly baked bread? Why did guests gravitate to the kitchen? What made the kitchen a natural gathering place in the home? Was it the warmth and good smells or was it because the kitchen was one of the larger rooms in the house? Sadly, the changing times are reflected in the diminished size of efficiency-conscious, convenience-laden, contemporary kitchens.

Gone are the large oil cloth or laminated-top kitchen tables and spacious counter tops that offered good, washable work surfaces for edible and non-edible projects. To set up non-edible projects, the solution is simple. Take to the kitchen floor. Spread a thick layer of newspaper for messy projects and then go to it!

A tray provides laptop workspace. If a tray is not available, a sturdy piece of cardboard covered with self-adhesive paper will do. It is amazing how the standbys in the kitchen become integral ingredients for homemade craft supplies.

Make It Yourself Modeling Compounds: There are two categories of modeling compounds. One is reusable when stored in an airtight bag. The other type is used as clay, then dried to make permanent ornaments, jewelry and other decorations.

Uncooked Reusable Modeling Compound
MATERIALS:
- 1 1/4 cups white all purpose flour
- 2/3 cup table salt
- 5 teaspoons powdered alum
- 1 tablespoon cooking oil
- 1 cup boiling water
- Several drops of green food coloring (optional)
- Kitchen utility spoon
- Large bowl

Directions: In a large bowl mix dry ingredients. Stir in oil. Pour in boiling water all at once and stir until dough becomes too stiff to stir. Gather the soft ball and knead until the dough is smooth and elastic.

Hint: To knead, round up the dough and push into the center with the heels of both hands. Fold over and push again. Repeat this until the dough is the desired consistency.

Cooked Reusable Modeling Compound
MATERIALS:
- 1 1/2 cups white all purpose flour
- 3/4 cup table salt
- 3 teaspoons cream of tartar
- 1 1/2 cup cold water
- 6 teaspoons cooking oil
- 1 teaspoon red food coloring
- 2 quart saucepan
- Kitchen utility spoon
- 2 cup measuring cup

Directions: Mix the dry ingredients in the saucepan. Combine the liquid ingredients in the measuring cup. Add the liquid to the dry ingredients and stir well until mixture is smooth. Cook mixture slowly over medium heat, stirring constantly. The mixture will thicken and when it becomes a pliable ball, remove the pan from the heat, turn the ball out onto a washable surface. When cool enough to handle, knead until smooth. Expect to knead for at least 5 minutes.

Store in an air-tight container or plastic bag.

Make It And Dry It Modeling Compound
MATERIALS:

    1 1/4 cups cornstarch

    2 cups baking soda

    1 1/3 cups cold water

    Large saucepan

    Kitchen utility spoon

Directions: Combine the dry ingredients in the saucepan. Gradually, add the water 1/3 of a cup at a time, stirring well. When all the water is added place over medium heat and stir constantly until the mixture resembles dough.

Mound up the mixture, let cool and knead until smooth. Cover unused portion with a moist paper towel and store in a plastic bag.

Suggested Uses For Modeling Compound:

Working with your hands, use the compound the way you would regular clay. Make snakes, bowls, balls, and people etc. Try pressing compound into plastic candy molds. Roll out with a rolling pin or pat out with your hands a portion of dough to desired thickness. Cut out with cookie cutter shapes or cut geometric shapes with a blunt table knife. Poke a hanging hole in the top of each shape.

Set aside to dry on a flat surface. When shape is dry, run string or ribbon through the hole and hang as a decoration or seasonal ornament. Paint if desired.

Hint: Let experience be the teacher here when determining how thick or thin to roll the modeling compound. Whatever the width, roll it uniformly so when the shapes are cut from it they will dry evenly. Too thick and the compound will absorb moisture; too thin and it will break.

Make It And Bake It Modeling Compound
MATERIALS:

    2 cups white all purpose flour

    1/2 cup table salt

    3/4 cup warm water

    Measuring cup

    Mixing bowl

Spoon

Baking pan with non-stick finish (When using a conventional baking pan, wipe lightly using a paper towel moistened with cooking oil.)

Directions: Measure flour and pour 1 1/2 cups into the mixing bowl, reserving the other 1/2 cup to add if needed while mixing. Stir the table salt into the flour. Pour in the warm water and stir the dough until it becomes too stiff to stir.

Directions to use: Sprinkle some of the flour on the work surface, place the lump of dough on the flour and knead. If the dough is too sticky work more flour into it while kneading.

Hint: Work quickly with this dough because it dries out. Work with a small portion at a time and keep the remainder of the dough in an air-tight container.

Suggested Uses For Make It And Bake It Modeling Compound:

Roll flat and cut with cookie cutters. Poke hole in top to create a decoration. Bake on a prepared baking pan in a 300 degree oven for 25 to 30 minutes or until golden brown.

To make beads, roll the compound into small balls. Poke a hole through the center of each ball with a large knitting needle or meat skewer. Bake the beads, bowls, and animals on the prepared baking pans for 45 minutes to an hour. Check for the golden color. The thicker the item, the longer the baking time.

Directions For Decorating Baked Art: Use model paint, water color paint, or felt tip marking pens to color. Seal colored or uncolored cutouts with acrylic floor wax or nail polish.

Hint: The seal serves as a preservative and prevents moisture absorption.

Gardening in the Kitchen

We all are observers. Children especially seem to derive great pleasure from watching things grow. At my house everyone was enthusiastic about planting and harvesting but mysteriously disappeared when weeding time came.

It's sad that not all children have the opportunity to plant an outdoor garden. The good news is everyone can have a tiny "kitchen garden" by sprouting carrot and pineapple tops, dried beans, or sweet potato eyes.

Sweet Potato Vine In Water
MATERIALS:
Sweet potato with eyes (looks like little bumps)
Glass jar
Water

Directions: Fill the jar half full with water. Put the potato in the water so that some of the eyes are above the water line. Set the jar in a place where there is good natural light, or on a sunny window sill. Add fresh water to the jar every day to keep the water level constant and before long a green leafy vine will grow and live for quite some time.

Hint: Some say the potato will sprout sooner if it has 24 hours of darkness.

Sweet Potato Vine In Sand
MATERIALS:
Sweet potato
Sand or potting soil
Shallow dish
Knife

Directions: Fill the shallow dish with moist sand. Cut the potato in half; place both halves cut side down and bring sand up around the cut edges, but do not cover the entire potato. Keep the sand moist as the vine grows.

Feathery Carrot Tops
MATERIALS:
Carrot
Shallow dish
Water
Knife

Directions: Fill the dish with water. Cut the top off the carrot leaving about 2 inches of carrot on it. Put the top in the dish of water. Watch it sprout and grow into feathery green foliage. Once the green growth is underway, the top can be transplanted into sand or potting soil and will root there.

Hint: For variety, try sprouting parsnip, turnip, or beet tops following the directions for the carrot top.

Sprouting A Dried Lima Bean
MATERIALS:

2 large dried lima beans

Blotting paper, cardboard wrapped with paper toweling, or other absorbent material

Clear, straight side drinking glass or jar

Scissors

Water

Directions: Cut the absorbent paper so it fits all the way around the inside of the glass. Position the paper in the glass. Tuck one lima bean between the glass and the paper on one side, turn the glass, and tuck the second lima bean between the paper and the side of the glass.

Carefully moisten the paper. Keep the paper moist for as long as the bean vine continues to grow.

The Hairy Runt
There is no accounting for why the children called this "The Hairy Runt." Perhaps this is one of those things that mothers aren't supposed to understand.

MATERIALS:

Very large baking potato

Potting Soil

Bird seed

Knife

Spoon

2 small buttons

4 2" cinnamon sticks or regular sticks broken into 2" lengths.

White craft glue

Directions: Slice off length-wise about 1/4 of the potato. Use the spoon to hollow out the inside of the potato leaving about 3/4 to 1 inch of potato flesh. Glue the button eyes on. Glue the legs or make small holes, and insert the legs.

Fill the cavity with potting soil. Spread a generous amount of bird seed in the soil. Stir with one finger to mix the seeds in with the soil. Add water and set The Hairy Runt in a sunny spot.

Hint: If you have bird seed but no potato, place a moistened sponge in a saucer, and sprinkle generously with bird seed. Keep the sponge moist by adding water to the saucer, not pouring directly on the seed. The sponge will absorb the water.

Peeling, Carving, And Printing With Fruits And Vegetables

Whom Will I Marry?
Does the letter the peel forms when thrown over the shoulder predict the marriage partner? Some say no while others believe it is so. In my youth, as the only girl in a family of six, it fell to me to peel many a potato for dinner or apples for applesauce. I had many opportunities to throw the unbroken peel over my shoulder, and it always landed as the initial "J."

At the time I knew no one with the initial "J." Then it happened. The special person who won my heart was called John.

MATERIALS:
1 unpeeled apple or potato
Paring knife

Directions: Peel the entire apple or potato in one long unbroken peel. Throw the peel over your shoulder and the initial that is formed by the peel is the initial of the one you will marry.

The peel is good for only one tossing!

Dried Apple Doll Head
As a carved apple dries and shrinks a delightfully wrinkled old granny or grandpa head emerges. In addition to using the dried apple head for doll making, consider using it for puppet making.

MATERIALS:
1 unblemished apple (Jonathan or Golden Delicious work well)
1 cup lemon juice
1 tablespoon salt
Small mixing bowl
Vegetable peeler
Small, sharp paring knife
Wire coat hanger

Directions: In the mixing bowl, dissolve the salt in the lemon juice. Peel the apple and dip it in the salty lemon juice to prevent excessive darkening while peeling and during the drying process.

Carve out two indentations which will become the eyes. Carve some of the apple away in the cheek area so a chunk emerges for the nose. Don't worry about carving a perfect nose, because during the drying process as the apple develops rubbery elasticity, the nose can be shaped by pulling it.

Under the nose area carve out a small smiling mouth. Drench the head one final time in the salty lemon juice. Unbend the wire coathanger and push the end through the apple head so it comes out the top. Hang the wire in a dry warm place. It should take about 2 to 3 weeks for the head to completely dry.

When the head is dry, use with your favorite doll body pattern or check the puppet-making section of this book for dowel body rod puppet instructions.

Hint: This is the best job in the world for the child with a tremendous desire to pinch, and we all know one! Have your pincher check the head every day, pinching the nose, tweaking the cheeks and chin to shape the face.

Carving Potato Pets
MATERIALS:
   1 large white potato
   Vegetable peeler
   Teaspoon (flatware not measuring spoon)
   Sharp paring knife

Directions: Select an animal picture, draw a reasonable facsimile of it or tap into imagination for the type animal to carve. Peel the potato. Use the teaspoon to hollow out areas and the knife for fine detail.

Directions To Cook The Potato Pet: Thoroughly wash the Potato Pet. Fill a saucepan with water deep enough to immerse the Potato Pet. Bring water to a boil and turn back to simmer. Check after 10 minutes.

The potato is cooked when a tooth pick can be easily inserted into the thickest part of the potato. Probe gently. To pierce with a fork might break the pet. Lift from the hot water with a long-handled slotted spoon. Serve a starfish or turtle on a bed of julienne carrots or French style green beans.

Hint: For a successful carving, begin with a star fish, fish or turtle. Avoid slender necks or thin appendages.

Amazing Apple Prints
MATERIALS:
1 small apple
Sharp knife
Paint
Construction paper
Shallow pan or saucer for paint
Protective covering for work surface

Directions: Put down protective covering. Pour small amount of paint in saucer. Cut apple in half horizontally, not from top to bottom. Look at the perfect star that is hiding in the center. Dip the star surface into the paint and press on to the construction paper.

Carving Potatoes For Printing

Small Hands Method:
The rule of thumb for this project could be "the small hand needs a big potato," simply because it is easier for a less dexterous, younger child to have a steady hand when there is something substantial to grip, not slip out of the fingers.
MATERIALS:
1 long baking potato
Sharp paring knife
Pencil
Protective covering for work surface

Directions For Carving A Star To Print: Cover the work surface. Do not peel the potato; instead cut off one end, leaving about 3/4 of the potato. Use the pencil to draw or trace the star pattern on the end of the potato. The pencil will make the grooves to follow when carving.

Use the paring knife to cut away extra potato tiny bits at a time, leaving the design raised between 1/2- and 3/4-inch above the remainder of the potato.

MATERIALS FOR PRINTING:
Potato design
Paint or India ink
Shallow saucer or paint dish
Manila paper, construction paper, typing paper

Directions: Using the unpeeled portion of the potato as the handle, dip the raised design in paint or India Ink and touch onto paper. Repeat if desired. With careful washing, the potato may be used with several colors of paint. Discard the potato when the printing is complete.

Hint: Make several designs to create greeting cards and seasonal wrapping paper. Print on fabric to make a wall hanging.

Designer Print Method
MATERIALS:
Small potato
Carving knife
Pattern or small metal cookie cutter
Paring knife
Protective covering for work surface

Directions: Peel the potato. Slice in 1-inch thick rounds; using cookie cutter cut the slices in desired shapes. If a star is selected, then cut the entire piece of potato in star shape. With the paring knife carve and discard unwanted pieces of potato to provide sharp definitive edges.

Cut more stars or other designs if desiring a repetitive or alternating pattern. Follow the printing directions for Small Hand Potato.

Soap Carving
MATERIALS:
1 bar bath soap
Paring knife
Pencil
Pattern
Tray to catch the soap scraps

Directions: Put the bar of soap on the tray and examine all sides of the soap for lettering. Remove all lettering by scraping the blade of the knife back and forth across the soap until the surface is smooth.

Follow the directions for Carving Potato Pets.

To smooth an area when the carving is completed, gently wet the portion of the soap to be reworked and rub with the forefinger.

Hint: Use up the soap scraps and avoid that disgusting jelly in the bottom of the soap dish. Fold a washcloth in half, stitch two sides. Fill the pouch with the soap-carving scraps. Stitch up the third side. The finished product is a terry cloth bath scrubber.

Friend To The Birds

There are more birds around in the winter than we realize, and they will appear at meal time if seed is put out on a regular basis. Bird lovers in apartments as well as houses may devise ingenious ways to feed the birds, dispelling misconceptions that seed must be placed on a bird feeder or sprinkled on the ground. Once again, let imagination leap the fence of traditional thinking.

Preparing bird treats is fun and so is watching the birds eat the treats. Each variety seems to have its eating preferences, not only in food selection, but in time of day or eating order. As with the case of cardinals in our yard, the male eats first.

We refer to the slate-colored juncos as snowbirds because they lead the way in feeding as the weather changes, just before the snow comes. An inexpensive bird book will help identify and give additional information about the feeding visitors. A spiral notebook serves well to record dates the birds appeared, unusual sightings etc. We had a three year stretch when no evening grosbeaks came to feed and a summer when all the hummingbirds disappeared in mid-July, finally to return in September.

An observation notebook may offer quiet reflective moments or settle arguments about which visitors came in which year, how many of what kind came during a big snow, etc. Spring observations could include the fancy struts of the males as they try to impress the females. Note the humorous escapades during twig, string and fuzz gathering for nest building.

From our observations inquisitive sparrows seem to be the most creative gatherers. There is one who haunts the clothes line in the spring and pulls ravelings from the frayed knees of my husband's jeans. This little bird is persistent about climbing in the necks of sweatshirts to gather fuzz. I have on occasion come into the family room to find my dog Josie sleeping peacefully on the couch while the pesky little sparrow is hopping around the family room rug pulling threads from the carpet. Evidently, she feels quite at home as she hops from the deck through Josie's doggie door. She knows the exit and if left undisturbed will hop out.

Take time to watch each summer day when the hatched baby birds are half grown, half feathered and try to fly. Something equally as interesting is to see how the nestlings protest, resist having to learn to feed themselves. I have seen baby robins refuse to peck and follow the mother making universal vocal comments that no mother enjoys.

In a matter of minutes migrating birds can strip berries from bushes and trees as they move in autumn on their way to winter quarters. Perhaps it is the curse/blessing of being an English teacher, but at times my bird notebook becomes a journal as I add lines of my own poetry or random lines of others.

As I watch the flocks of birds, the last four lines of William Cullen Bryant's "To A Waterfowl" circle around my brain:

He who, from zone to zone,
Guides through the boundless sky thy certain flight,
In the long way that I must tread alone,
Will lead my steps aright.

Birdwatching from inside is fun, but it has drawbacks. One slight movement will startle the birds, and most will fly away not to return until the next meal. If more than one person is looking out the window, there is elbowing, jockeying for position. The following viewing method really works.

Bird Peeking Station
MATERIALS:
   Poster board
   Scissors
   Pencil
   Tape
   1 quarter

Directions: Cut the poster board to fit the window. Trace around the quarter in three different spots on the poster board and cut out the holes. Secure the poster board in the window, using small pieces of tape if necessary, to hold in place. Peek through the holes at the birds.

Hint: Do not wait until the birds arrive to feed before putting the peek station in place. Have everything ready so the birds do not detect movement. Enjoy!

Bird Feasts

These are alternative methods to the usual "put the seed in the feeder" feeding.

Fruit Delight

Those who do the stringing enjoy nibbling the treats as they work. Remember before this disposable era an adage to which people adhered – "Waste not want not?" This is a "natural" way to put those aging oranges or bruised apples we all shove to the back of the bottom shelf in the refrigerator to good use.

MATERIALS:

    1 orange
    1 apple
    Popped, plain popcorn
    Heavy duty thread
    Darning or other large eye needle
    String
    Scissors
    Thimble
    Knife
    Cutting board

Directions: Slice the apple and the orange in rounds and cut each round into fourths. Thread the needle with a 24-inch length of thread. Longer strings may tangle or knot during the process. If a longer treat string is desired, leave a small length of string at each end and tie the shorter finished strings together.

Begin the stringing with an orange wedge and tie the orange to the end of the string as a "stopper." String the items in random or predetermined order using the thimble to protect the "needle pushing" finger. Tie the last item in the same manner as the beginning item to complete the treat string.

Hang the completed treat string from sash to sash outside the window and view the visitors to the bird buffet through the peeking station. Be patient. Because they are unaccustomed to seeing the Fruit Treat, the birds may take a while before they are brave enough to try it. As word spreads, the birds will come. Use the long strings also as garlands on trees or tall shrubbery.

Hint: Keep a moist cloth available because sometimes the workers get sticky hands.

Bird Beads
MATERIALS:

    Fresh cranberries
    Stale bread
    Heavy thread
    Needle
    Thimble

Directions: Follow directions for stringing Fruit Delight.

Bird Brunch
MATERIALS:

    6 tablespoons of crunchy peanut butter
    1 cup bird seed
    2 cups yellow cornmeal
    1/2 cup finely crushed stale bread crumbs
    1/2 cup melted vegetable shortening
    Small straw heart wreath or 4 pine cones
    String or yarn for hanging straw wreath, pine cones
    Table knife
    Mixing bowl
    Cake pan
    Protective covering for work surface

Directions: In a mixing bowl combine bird seed, cornmeal and bread crumbs. Stir in melted shortening. Mix the peanut butter into the mixture, using hands to blend ingredients. Spread the mixture on all parts of the straw heart.

Pour additional bird seed (add sunflower seeds if available) into cake tin and press one side of the heart into the seeds. Turn the heart and repeat on the other side. Tie yarn in each of the arcs of the heart to create a loop hanger. Hang the heart where you can watch the birds feast.

This heart may be "refilled."

Variation: Work yarn twice around a pine cone to form a hanging loop. Spread mixture on pine cones and roll in additional seed. Hang the pine cone in a place where you can watch the birds feast.

Treats From The Kitchen

Remember when we used to get the kitchen floor so sticky we were glued down and couldn't walk? To this day when my grown children get together one topic they always recount is group efforts in the kitchen. We had good times, created tasty treats (emphasis was not on nutrition), and eventually cleaned up. The important outcome is that they remember the good times elbow to elbow at the kitchen counter.

Now as they establish their own homes, they carry on the kitchen traditions, sticky floors and all.

To avoid burns, adults should take an active part in preparation of the recipes that involve heating ingredients and pouring hot sugar syrups.

Rock Candy (Amber)
INGREDIENTS AND MATERIALS:
 4 cups brown sugar
 1 cup water
 String
 Wooden meat skewer or craft stick
 Pint canning jar
 Saucepan

Directions: Measure two lengths of string, allowing for enough string to tie around the stick and to reach the bottom of the glass jar. Place the jar on a heat-resistant surface.

Combine 2 cups of brown sugar and all the water in the saucepan. Heat on medium and stir until sugar dissolves. Add another cup of brown sugar and again, stir until all the sugar is dissolved.

Stir in the final cup of brown sugar and continue to heat the mixture until the liquid becomes clear amber color. Slowly and carefully pour the hot liquid into the jar. Dangle the strings in the liquid, and rest the wooden skewer on across the mouth of the jar.

Within about 6 to 8 hours the first candy crystals will appear on the string. The crystal forming process may take several days.

Variation: To make clear crystal rock candy, substitute white sugar for brown sugar and follow the same directions.

Popcorn Balls
INGREDIENTS AND MATERIALS:
  3 quarts popped corn
  1 1/3 cup white sugar
  1 cup water
  1/4 cup light corn syrup
  1/4 teaspoon salt
  1/2 teaspoon cider vinegar
  Deep saucepan with lid
  Candy thermometer (optional)
  Large, deep bowl
  Long-handled wooden spoon

Directions: Combine all ingredients except popcorn in saucepan and stir until all the sugar is dissolved. Cover the saucepan, gradually increasing heat, bringing the mixture to a boil.

Boil for 3 minutes. Uncover and continue to cook without stirring until syrup forms a brittle ball (275-290 degrees on a candy thermometer) when dropped in cool water. Put popcorn in a deep bowl. With great caution, remove saucepan from heat and pour the very hot syrup over popcorn.

With the wooden spoon, carefully, gently stir the popcorn until it is coated. When the popcorn is cool enough to handle, lightly butter your hands and shape into balls.

Wrap the balls in plastic wrap to maintain freshness.

Caramel Popcorn Balls
INGREDIENTS AND MATERIALS:
  6 cups popped corn
  4 heaping teaspoons margarine
  1 1/2 cups brown sugar
  1/3 cup water
  Saucepan with cover
  Deep bowl
  Wooden spoon
  Plastic wrap

Directions: Follow cooking directions for popcorn balls. However, the caramel syrup should reach soft ball stage (238 degrees on a candy thermometer) rather than crackling hard ball stage when dropped in cold water.

Chocolate Lovers' Popcorn Balls
INGREDIENTS AND MATERIALS:
9 cups popped, unsalted popcorn
1/2 cup marshmallow topping
6 ounces semi-sweet chocolate bits
1 tablespoon water
1 teaspoon vanilla
9" X 13" baking pan
Double boiler

Directions: After greasing the baking pan, fill it with the popped corn. Melt chocolate bits over boiling water in the top of a double boiler. Stir constantly to encourage smooth, uniform melting.

When the chocolate is soft, stir marshmallow topping into melted chocolate and continue to heat over boiling water stirring until mixture is smooth. Stir in water and vanilla.

Pour the chocolate marshmallow mixture over the corn, mixing thoroughly to coat all the popcorn. Lightly grease hands and shape popcorn into balls.

Molasses Popcorn Balls
INGREDIENTS AND MATERIALS:
3 quarts popped corn
1 cup white sugar
1/3 cup water
1/3 cup unsulphured molasses
3 tablespoons of butter or margarine
3/4 teaspoon of vanilla
Saucepan with lid
Candy thermometer (optional)
Wooden spoon
Large bowl
Plastic wrap

Directions: Combine all the ingredients except popcorn and vanilla in the saucepan. Follow the cooking directions for plain Popcorn Balls. When the syrup reaches the crackling hard ball stage (275 to 290 degrees on a candy thermometer) when dropped in cold water, remove from the heat and carefully stir vanilla into the hot mixture.

Pour the hot syrup slowly over popcorn, stirring the popcorn until it is completely coated. When the popcorn is cool enough to handle, dampen hands with water and shape into balls. Wrap in plastic wrap to maintain freshness.

Tropical Delight Popcorn Candy Crunch
INGREDIENTS AND MATERIALS:
    3 quarts of popped corn
    1/2 cup Spanish peanuts
    1/2 assorted chopped dried fruit (pineapple, apricots, raisins)
    1/2 cup margarine
    1/2 cup honey
    Roasting pan
    Small saucepan
    Jelly roll or broiler pan

Directions: Place the roasting pan filled with popcorn, peanuts, and dried fruit in an oven preheated to 250 degrees. Lightly oil the jelly roll pan.

Melt margarine in the small saucepan, then stir in the honey. Increase the oven temperature to 325 degrees, remove the roasting pan from the oven, and pour the margarine and honey mixture over the popcorn mixture, stirring well to coat all the dry ingredients.

Turn the mixture into the oiled jelly roll pan, spreading it evenly and into all four corners of the pan. Return to oven. Check the popcorn after 10 minutes. If it is crisp, remove. Allow 5 minutes more baking time for extra crunchy.

Let the crunch cool, then break by hand or use an oiled knife to cut into chunks.

Molasses Mint Taffy
INGREDIENTS AND MATERIALS:
    1 cup molasses
    2 teaspoons cider vinegar
    3/4 cup sugar
    1 tablespoon baking soda
    2 tablespoons margarine
    1/2 to 1 teaspoon peppermint extract
    Pinch of salt
    Saucepan
    Wooden spoon
    9" X 11" baking pan

Directions: Grease the baking pan with margarine. Combine molasses, vinegar and sugar in saucepan. Cook over medium heat, stirring constantly to prevent sticking or burning until it reaches crackling hard ball stage when dropped in cold water (275 to 290 degrees on a candy thermometer).

Remove from heat and add soda, margarine, peppermint and salt. Carefully, because the mixture is very hot, stir briskly until foamy. Pour the molasses mixture into the baking pan. Let the mixture set up in the pan until it is cool enough to handle then cut it in half and pull 1/2 at a time.

Pull the mixture repeatedly until it looses its stickiness, firms up and takes on a lighter color. Cut or break into individual size pieces and wrap individual pieces in plastic kitchen wrap.

Apple Leather
INGREDIENTS AND MATERIALS:
>   3 cups applesauce
>   1/2 cup sugar
>   1/2 teaspoon cinnamon
>   1/4 teaspoon nutmeg
>   Confectioners sugar
>   Finely chopped walnuts (optional)
>   9" X 11" baking pan

Directions: Mix the ingredients and spread about 1/2 inch thick in the baking pan. Bake about 3 hours in a very slow oven (250 degrees). When applesauce looks dry and leathery it is finished baking. Remove from the oven and sprinkle the top with confectioners sugar.

Spread a layer of confectioners sugar on the counter or on a cutting board. Turn the apple leather out on the sugared surface with the "top" side becoming the "under" side. Sprinkle top side with confectioners sugar and walnuts.

Start at one end and roll into a long roll. Dust with more confectioners sugar and slice into small rounds.

Gingerbread Men
INGREDIENTS AND MATERIALS:
>   1 cup white sugar
>   1/2 cup margarine
>   2 eggs
>   1/2 cup molasses

3 1/2 cups unbleached flour
2 teaspoons baking soda
1 1/2 teaspoons powdered ginger
1/2 teaspoon powdered cloves
1/2 teaspoon powdered cinnamon
1/4 teaspoon grated nutmeg
1/4 teaspoon grated allspice
1/4 teaspoon salt
Cinnamon red dot candies
Raisins
Rolling pin
Ungreased cookie sheets
Medium size gingerbread man cookie cutter
Spatula

Directions: Combine sugar, margarine, butter, eggs and molasses and beat until well mixed. Add dry ingredients to sugar mixture and mix until dough is smooth and stiff. Cover and refrigerate 6 hours or overnight.

Preheat oven to 375 degrees. Sprinkle pastry cloth or work surface, rolling pin and hands with flour. Keep extra flour handy for additional dusting of cookie cutter, work surface and hands. Work with a small amount of dough and keep the rest in the refrigerator.

Roll the dough to about 1/8 inch thickness and cut out gingerbread men. Place them on cookie sheet, give each one a cinnamon candy heart and two raisin eyes. If using a small gingerbread man cutter, consider currants or cutting the raisins in half or quarters for smaller eyes.

Approximate baking time is 6 to 8 minutes. These cookies are finished when they turn light brown, so begin checking at 6 minutes. Yield: Approximately 8 dozen medium gingerbread boys.

Gingerbread cookies store well in an air tight tin, freeze well and ship well.

Hint: This is a good recipe to use for gingerbread hearts on St. Valentine's Day.

Smash Cookies
INGREDIENTS AND MATERIALS:
1/2 cup margarine
1 cup granulated white sugar
1 egg (well beaten before adding)

1 teaspoon vanilla
1 tablespoon milk
1 1/2 cups unbleached flour
1 teaspoon baking powder
Pinch of salt
Extra granulated sugar
Cookie sheet
Flat-bottomed glass
Wire rack or paper towels

Directions: In a mixing bowl combine margarine, sugar, egg, vanilla, and milk and beat well. Add the dry ingredients and mix well. Cover dough with plastic wrap and refrigerate for about 3 hours until completely chilled.

Preheat the oven to 350 degrees. Lightly grease cookie sheet. Fill a small saucer with granulated sugar. Make balls of dough about the size of a small walnut. Roll each dough ball in the granulated sugar and place on the cookie sheet leaving spread space between each ball.

When the sheet is full of dough balls, dip the flat bottom of a glass in the granulated sugar and smash a dough ball. Dip the bottom of the glass in the sugar before each dough ball is "smashed."

Baking time is 8 to 10 minutes. The cookies are done when lightly browned around the edges. Remove immediately from the cookie sheet and place on a wire rack or paper towel for cooling.

Hint: These cookies cling tenaciously to the sheet if there is a delay in removing them. The simple solution is to run the sheet, cookies and all back in the oven for a very brief time to release the cookies. The same reheat method works for ease in washing the sugar from the cookie sheet.

Lemonade
INGREDIENTS AND MATERIALS:

2 cups granulated sugar
2 cups water
1 large lemon
Lemon squeezer
Saucepan
1-quart glass jar

Directions: Make sugar syrup by stirring the sugar into the water in a saucepan over medium heat. Stir until sugar is dissolved. Increase heat until sugar mixture begins to boil; let boil for 5 minutes.

Pour the syrup in the glass jar, cool and store in the refrigerator. Use this chilled syrup for fresh lemonade, orangeade, and grapeade.

To Make One Glass Of Lemonade: Squeeze the lemon to make 1/3 cup of juice. In a tall glass mix lemon juice with 4 tablespoons of sugar syrup. Add water to make the glass 3/4 full. Taste and add more sugar syrup, a teaspoon at a time, until the desired sweetness is achieved.

Add ice and garnish with lemon peel, mint leaves etc.

Hint: For a surprise, freeze a mint leaf or maraschino cherry in each ice cube.

Mother's Homemade Hot Chocolate
INGREDIENTS AND MATERIALS:
    1 1/2 squares unsweetened baking chocolate
    1/4 cup sugar
    3 cups milk
    1 cup boiling water
    1 teaspoon vanilla
    1/4 teaspoon cinnamon
    Dash of salt
    Double boiler
    2-quart saucepan
    Wooden spoon
    Egg beater or whisk

Directions: In the saucepan scald milk by heating it to just under the boiling point. You can tell when the milk reaches the "ready" point by watching milk at the edge of the pan for signs of "simmer bubbles."

While the milk is heating, melt chocolate over boiling water in the double boiler. Add sugar, cinnamon, and salt to the chocolate. Slowly stir in 1/2 cup boiling water. When that is smooth and well blended, stir in the other half of the boiling water.

Continue cooking and stirring the chocolate mixture for 5 minutes. Stir carefully while adding the chocolate mixture slowly into the hot milk. With the egg beater or whisk whip the hot chocolate until it is foamy.

Serve in a mug topped with a marshmallow.

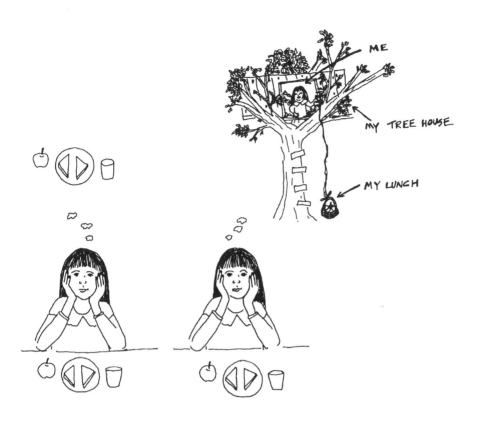

What Is Using
Your Imagination Anyway?

Want to drive me crazy?

Say to a child, within my hearing, "Oh, you're just imagining things."

"You are letting your imagination run away with you."

Or worst of all, "Use your imagination, you'll think of something!" One might as well say, "Here's a nice flat soccer ball – now, go kick it and have fun!"

For me "the imagination" is that sacred, secret, mysterious place in each of us where glorious, wondrous ideas come to life, and all things are possible. Rapunzel lets down her golden hair, animals have conversations, dolls give parties and move about the house when everyone is sleeping; I sit again in the sun on the fender of my grandfather's tractor, holding on to his belt, dodging grasshoppers as we mow the upper meadow.

In bleak winter as I stand among my sleeping herbs, I see their blossoms, head-heavy with bees and butterflies, and yes, wishes come true in my imagination.

Think about opening a trunk in the attic, peeking into a musty tool shed, reaching to the back of a drawer, and you'll locate your imagination. If you accept, nurture, practice, and love your imaginative force, it will offer creative enrichment and satisfaction for you and those around you.

It is not my intent to use imagination as a regular means of escape from reality, nor do I want to offend people traumatized by unfortunate events and personal tragedies. Sometimes these victims are plagued by fears, imagined or real. Perhaps, sensitive understanding of such circumstances may help the one in stress keep the real world in perspective by encouraging a "healthy" imagination. In positive circumstances an imagination is a wonderful thing, and for those who will let it soar, it is a delight and a treasure.

When a child or an adult recognizes the imagination as a welcome, positive and natural faculty, then unpleasant things attributed to "overactive imagination" generally fall into perspective and lose credibility.

I remember that when my brother Terry was about four years old, he dreaded bedtime because he was easily startled from sleep by (to others!) benign and ordinary noises. When he feared sleeping and waking to such sounds as the heater's cracks and thumps, my mother didn't put him off by saying, "Nothing's wrong, it's just your imagination." She brought in a revolving Christmas tree lamp which dusted the walls of his room with soft light patterns. For several nights in the flickering light she sat on the bed beside him, encouraged him to discuss all the possibilities. On his own, with his imagination, Terry covered the gamut from drooling monsters to attacking indians moving down the ravine and across the creek.

Together he and our mother used their imaginations and came up with some outlandish and humorous possibilities. When he understood that the old radiator in his room made "heat bangs," as he called them, he wore his holster set to bed and shot the heat bangs with his "sixshooters." Terry didn't deny reality, rather he accepted it and through imaginative, creative problem-solving took control of the situation.

Terry's story is one of innocence. What has happened? Today, a surprising number of children have unsettling personal agendas, commit acts of violence, tell lies of great consequence to attain their goals. The days of reporting to the teacher, "The dog ate my homework," are gone.

And conversely, so are the days of listening. We hear what we want to hear, rushing the speaker to get to the point, projecting, formulating an answer before the speaker has made the point. Sometimes the speaker doesn't have a point or want a solution, just a good listener.

Being inattentive, we fail to assess situations and as a result, try to force our opinions. The lack of communication snowballs, and discussion becomes a shouting match.

How do we as parents, grandparents and teachers encourage and reinforce positive communication and listening skills? Certainly not by sentencing the listener to a chair, wagging a finger in his/her face and saying, "Now you listen to me!"

How about storytelling?

Even the smelliest old fish story about the big one that got away has new life breathed into it when told to a good listener by a clever storyteller. Think of it! We could revive vanishing listening skills and diminishing imaginations by encouraging storytelling. The possibilities are endless, through imagination. After all, didn't Peter Pan teach Wendy to fly?

Why not begin within your family and develop the "oral tradition," passing along stories special to those around you? Children love to hear about themselves, but don't forget they have their own perspective on family stories. Imagine the story Wendy could tell about flying and how her brothers, John and Michael, must have viewed it!

As opportunities arise, storytelling translates beautifully into classroom activities. Be a listener as well as a teller. At the onset, the content is not as important as the words flowing. Stories are not quarterly reports or academic lectures – don't worry about inaccuracies in your story or in others'. Celebrate the spoken word!

Since I am of Scotch-Irish ancestry and grew up in a household of storytellers, I've needed no motivation. If storytelling and family traditions have not been your "thing," you might feel a bit awkward launching into a family storytelling project. Go for it! What have you got to lose?

Where in the world is the best location to tell a story? Where are you now? Where and when is there an opportunity, perhaps a need? Stories are entertainment. What do you do when the charcoal grill is slow to start, and everyone is starving? Tell a story.

When the trip to the beach is rained out, spread out the beach blanket on the living room floor, inflate the rafts, scatter a few shells if you have them, serve a picnic and tell stories. An outlandish yarn will help take a sick-in-bed person's mind off illness, help pass the time during an endless wait in the dentist's office, airport, creeping traffic.

In the evening a quiet story will relax the listener, sometimes the teller, into sleep. Consider how Henry Wadsworth Longfellow, one of the "Fireside Poets," thought the day should wind down in the closing lines from his poem, "The Day is Done."

And lend to the rhyme of the poet
  The beauty of thy voice.
And the night shall be filled with music,
  And the cares, that infest the day,
Shall fold their tents like the Arabs,
  And silently steal away.

Here are a few hints that have worked for me. These suggestions may not turn anyone into a polished professional, but will give you a point of reference if you are one of the folks that say, "I would, but I don't know how!"

1. Since this story is spoken, not written, keep it short and simple and without elaborate details and pretentious vocabulary. A beginning listener (young or old) may get distracted by burdensome details or big words, and miss the heart of the story.

2. Eye contact will keep the listener involved in the story.

3. Tell the story in your own voice, using inflection, sighs, or pauses for emphasis. Creating a variety of voices for characters in your story can be confusing to the listener and a nuisance to you.

4. Enjoy the story you are telling, and your listener will enjoy it too.

Recently, after the death of my parents, although still reasonably young I suddenly found myself the oldest member of my family. With this new position came what I consider a serious trust, the responsibility of keeping alive and passing along the family stories. Every now and then there is a word, a phrase, a sentence that literally spins me around. Lines from East Tennessee playwright and poet Jo Carson hit home. The following lines from "# 54," the final selection in the collection of monologues and dialogues, *Stories I Ain't Told Nobody Yet* reaffirmed my passionate, personal mission.

I'd rather you come back now and got my stories.
I've got whole lives of stories that belong to you.
I could fill you up with stories,
stories I ain't told nobody yet,
stories with your name, your blood in them.
Ain't nobody gonna hear them if you don't
and you ain't gonna hear them unless you get back home.
When I am dead, it will not matter
how hard you press your ear to the ground.

Tell and retell your family stories to shore up the foundation of the heart. Then you will always be able to find your way home.

Folktales

Once you settle in the groove of telling family stories, expand your horizons. Look around for traditional folktales and retell them. There are certain schools of thought that contend some folktales are too violent and children will be frightened, possibly receiving a negative message. That is the beauty of retelling the traditional tales. Keep the basic story line and alter it to suit the needs of your audiences.

"What happens if we don't know any folktales?" That's what my two classes of pleasant but not always motivated and sometimes under-achieving 11th graders said to me as we considered involvement and activities with a small class of 8-year-olds.

What about The Runaway Gingerbread Man, Hansel and Gretel, Rapunzel? As my students read and finally wrote their own versions. for the 8-year-olds, the students were astonished to discover that around the world there exist at least 600 versions of Cinderella. They found that wonderful stories – and variations – spring from ethnic, cultural, religious, and geographical sources.

We can all take a lesson, and encouragement, from my students. They simplified matters by arranging folktales into three categories: myths, legends and fables.

Myths

These are stories developed long ago to explain how the world and man developed. Often myths are the basis for customs, religious practices, festivals and celebrations. Myths usually involve supernatural beings and occurrences.

We generally think first of the Greek and Roman gods and goddesses. Can you experience Valentine's day without the Roman Cupid? Do you know Apollo, the Greek god of light who, as myths tell us, drove his chariot across the heavens creating the sunrise, bringing sunset?

Then there is the Greek Zeus (his Roman counterpart is Jupiter) whose domain is the sky. He is credited with weather conditions, fair as well as stormy with thunder and lightning. Hold on! Didn't you have a thunderstorm explained to you in less than scientific terms? I did. During severe thunderstorms, my dad told me Thor was throwing lightning bolts and thunder balls. Who is Thor anyway?

He is part of Norse folklore. This brings me to another important point. The Greeks and Romans appear to have cornered the mythological market. But notice theirs are not the only myths. All cultures are rich with explanations as to how and why things happen.

Examine Native American myths such as, "The Walam Olum," the Delawares' explanation of the world's creation. The Navajos have a tender, lyrical story about the creation of man and woman. A fascinating Native American tale involves the raven and its experience with fire. It is not a bird but the dog who is an important figure in African myths that explain the origin of fire. The spider and the hare also have their place in African mythology to explain why things happen.

Legends

Occasionally, this type of story is confused with the myth. In some respects the two are similar. Like myths, legends involve a particular person and are told as if the person existed, and the story were true.

As a rule, legends are set in the real world in fairly recent times, as opposed to thousands of years ago. On closer examination, we may see how legends are a reflection of cultural values. Consider the perennial Halloween favorite, Washington Irving's classic story of life in the Hudson River Valley, the struggle of brainy Ichabod Crane versus brawny Brom Bones to win the beautiful Katrina Van Tassel, in *The Legend of Sleepy Hollow.*

America's folklore is rich with "legendary" figures such as Pecos Bill, Paul Bunyan, John Henry, and, of late, Bigfoot. Although Johnny Appleseed, Daniel Boone and Davy Crockett were real, their stories surpass their actual accomplishments.

A figure who can not be overlooked in American folklore is that clever trickster named Jack, hero of the Appalachian "Jack Tales" whose exploits have fostered the careers of several professional story-tellers. Brer Rabbit is another sly character who bounds through African-American folktales.

Across the border Pancho Villa rides through Mexican stories. Once again, consider Native American explanation stories. The story, sometimes attributed to the Choctaw Indians, of how Spanish moss came to be is a wonderful legend.

Fables

In these very short stories, the main characters are talking animals with human traits. Each story is designed to teach a lesson, moral, or provide "food for thought." At the mention of fables, we are conditioned to think "The Tortoise and The Hare," or "The Fox and the Grapes."

Don't stop there. Certainly, dig deeper into Aesop's fables, but look to other sources too. Twentieth Century American writer and humorist James Thurber has added his brand of satirical fables, *Fables for Our Time,* to American literature.

Storytelling And Beyond

Sometimes children get fidgety, interrupt or want to take an active part in storytelling. Be flexible! One way to involve the child is to determine a key word, perhaps the name of the main character. Every time the character's name is mentioned the child claps once. When the child gets the idea and anticipates the name, pause rather than saying the name. The pause is the key for the child to clap. Have the child tell the story, pausing for you to clap.

Some children enjoy illustrated stories. Resurrect the flannel board. "Flannel board" isn't in your vocabulary? Cover a sturdy piece of cardboard with solid color flannel or felt. Cut out shapes like trees, animals, houses, and people of flannel or felt. Flannel adheres to flannel and can be rearranged to suit any story. Something that works well, is conveniently stored, and travels without mess is a shoe box with a flannel-lined top. Keep the figures in the shoe box, and nothing gets dirty, sucked up in the vacuum cleaner or lost.

Using A Flannel Board

1. A common use is for the storyteller or "helper" to put the figures up as they are mentioned in the story. As the story advances, the figures are changed and rearranged.

2. Another variation on the flannel board works when there are several listeners. Begin the story, add a flannel figure, and have a listener advance the story by giving information about the new shape on the board. Traditional stories take interesting twists when the imagination is at work.

3. Children enjoy challenging adults. Have a young listener arrange the flannel figures without giving any explanation. It is up to the storyteller to create a story with the figures given. To remedy a lagging story, especially if your idea-tank is running low, you can ask the child to make a comment, rearrange or add new figures. If you have dug yourself into a storytelling hole, you can always say the words that kids love to hear: "You really stumped me this time!"

Using Shadows

Remember what occurred in that 60-second corridor of time while your seventh-grade social studies teacher had trouble threading the filmstrip into the projector?

There was always one person who jumped up and tried to look directly into the projector. The teacher would say, "Don't look into the projector, you'll burn your retinas!" as the class laughed at the image of the student projected on the wall. The rebuffed student invariably made shadow spiders to scare the girls and using both hands staged a dog fight with sound effects.

Hand shadows are fun and may be used as story telling devices. Often a spontaneous homemade story develops as the images appear. On other occasions, shadow figures may be invented to enhance the story. Please be advised that serious shadow makers usually develop a mind-boggling collection of hand positions.

How To Get Started: Use a high intensity light or a lamp with 100 watt bulb. Use a solid background such as white poster board, white cloth, a window shade or plain wall on which to cast the shadow. Work three to four feet from the light source to cast a small, well-defined shadow.

When entertaining a small group, perhaps in a classroom setting, an alternative method of shadow-casting may be feasible. Using thumb tacks, hang a white sheet taut across the top half of a doorway. The sheet is the screen for the shadows. Thumbtack a beach towel or heavy fabric across the bottom half of the doorway or use a card table to block the light from showing through. This way shadow makers or puppeteers have space to maneuver behind the sheet and still remain invisible.

Experiment, create, and practice hand shadows.

Some Shadow Figures:
SNAPPING 'GATOR
Place palms of hands together with fingers extended. Open and close outstretched hands to emulate a snapping 'gator.
FLYING BIRD
Work with palms of hands towards the light source. With open hands, place thumbs so that right thumb rests on left thumb and the fingers extend out on each side in wing formation. Starting position is with fingers cupped, thumbs overlapping. Gently open and close fingers in a wave. Your bird will appear to fly.
BUTTERFLY
With palms away from the light source make an "X" with thumbs, right over left. Keep hands rigid, fingers together to form the wings.

JUMBO ELEPHANT

On the left hand extend the pointer and little finger. Bend the thumb into the palm, while letting the third and fourth fingers droop. Cup the right hand with thumb touching the other fingers of the hand. Rest the cupped right hand on top of the left hand to complete the elephant.

WATCHDOG

Make the left hand into a fist, thumb dangling down. Make the right hand into a fist, thumb up. Place the right fist on top of the left fist and adjust until you get a dog head that pleases. Wiggle the left thumb to make the dog bark.

OLD BUZZARD

Fold the third, fourth and fifth fingers of the right hand into the palm. Make a pinching action of thumb and forefinger. Tip hand so that knuckle of forefinger faces towards the light source. Pull the thumb back and adjust to a position between the first and second knuckle to create the drooping beak.

Shadow Puppets

Where and when shadow puppets were developed is unclear. According to some historians, shadow puppets were created in the ancient Orient to retell live-theater dramas. Others say shadow puppets made from thin leather are of middle eastern origin, meant for spiritual enrichment as dramas of religious significance, and were cast upon tent walls.

Shadow puppets are fun, quick, and easy to make. Few materials are needed. Best of all, there is very little frustration in creating the puppet, because nothing is seen but the silhouette. Most shapes can be taped to a pencil, craft stick, or sturdy wire.

This discussion addresses puppets in general, shadow puppets specifically: Children and adults drop inhibitions and become honest, bold, witty and often tenderly sensitive when projecting unseen through the persona of a puppet.

Puppetry is a wonderfully safe method to release feelings. Long ago, when I taught nursery school, a bouncy four-year-old boy was noticeably not himself for several days. He told me the family dog had died, and they had adopted a little puppy. We were doing something with puppets, and quite unexpectedly it came out through his puppet how heart-heavy he was because he believed his father had killed the family dog.

In truth the father had the sad task of taking the beloved, critically-ill dog to the veterinarian to be put to sleep. Although it had been explained to the child, he didn't quite understand and as a result he was angry. Years later when I graduated to high school teaching, the same young man appeared in my class. Evidently the day the puppet spilled the beans still lives in his memory. He remembers the flooding personal relief when the puppet told everybody about his father's deed.

Making A Simple Shadow Puppet
MATERIALS:
> Black poster board or other dark, heavy paper
> Patterns (May be drawn free hand, cut from catalogs, magazines, or made from cookie cutter shapes such as animals or a gingerbread man.)
> Poster board or 4" X 6" index cards
> Pencil
> Clear tape
> Sharp scissors
> Pencil, craft stick, or heavy wire

Directions: Make patterns for the shapes you will need in your play. Trace the patterns on poster board or large index cards. Cut them out. Tape a stick onto the back of each puppet. Do not draw features because only the outline of the figure will be seen. Create the grand performance behind the sheet screen.

Puppets
Although there are many varieties of puppets and string controlled marionettes, only quick and easy-to-construct puppets are considered here. I have not overlooked but rather chosen not to include styrofoam or papier-mache head puppets, marionettes, and more sophisticated rod puppets. These take time, patience, and skill. If you develop a keen interest in puppet construction, they are worth exploring.

My intent is to get the puppet enthusiasm rolling. Should you want additional information, go with a happy heart to the library or craft center knowing you can immerse yourself in colorful, beautifully detailed puppet books. Following the ideas for simple puppets are some ideas for using them and suggestions for constructing puppet stages.

For as long as stories have been told, lessons taught, puppets have been popular. Early records show that touring puppet shows entertained the wealthy in castles and commoners in the market places of antiquity. During the spread of Christianity, when very few people could read, puppets were used to teach and illustrate Bible stories.

There is what I call a Punch and Judy Syndrome which develops as children slip fingers into puppet heads and bodies. Remember Punch and Judy, the perennial quarrelsome couple? Their famous or infamous altercations have endeared them to Italian, French and English audiences through the centuries. Poor Punch continually blunders in such a way that Judy resorts to soundly pounding him with a little club.

Talk yourself blue with puppet protocol in preparation for play, but in the hands of children, puppets with mouths immediately bite, and the puppets with arms grab and pull. I have found a "most of the time" workable solution to puppet madness. This solution also addresses the "I don't know what to make" words out of the child's mouth when presented with puppet making.

Begin with your own already constructed, ready to decorate, fingers and hands! There is less temptation to grab with a painted finger or hand. Evidently advertisers realize the public is entertained by painted fingers and hands because finger puppets are perennial favorites in television commercials.

Making And Decorating Puppets

Please don't look at this list and assume that because you don't have every item you can't make puppets! This very basic supply list contains materials used for the various puppets suggested in this section. If you don't have everything, relax, improvise and most of all have fun!

MATERIALS:

Assortment of buttons, sequins, beads etc.
Assortment of stickers (stars, loose leaf reinforcement "o's")
Brown paper lunch bags
Construction paper (white and colored)
Cardboard or poster board
Cotton balls
Fabric scraps (felt, cotton and other sturdy fabric)
Face paint (may be purchased from arts and crafts centers or school supply stores)
Felt tip fine line and broad line marking pens (water soluble, nontoxic variety)

Glue (white craft glue and fabric glue)
Model paint and brushes
Needle and thread
Pencil (#2 soft)
Paper plates
Scissors (dressmaker shears and pinking shears)
Tape
Wooden spoon
Yarn, ribbon, and string scraps

Painted Fingers And Hands As Puppets
Thumbkin
MATERIALS:
Water soluble, non-toxic felt tip pen (red and black)
Colored facial tissue

Directions: Draw a face on the fleshy part of the thumb. Wrap the tissue around the thumb leaving space for the face to peek out. Wiggle the thumb to bring the puppet to life.

Hands As Puppets
MATERIALS:
Three colors of face paint (available at teacher supply stores, arts and crafts stores)

Directions: For a full front view, paint the facial features on the palm of the hand. Paint the fingers and spread them as hair. For a side view puppet, paint the thumb as a nose with the mouth at the base of the thumb. Have only one eye and eyebrow in the palm.

The four fingers become the hair. The "hair fingers" may be loosely bound together and tied with a yarn bow.

Fingers
MATERIALS:

Non-toxic, water soluble felt tip pens

Directions: Use the palm-side tips of fingers for the faces. Draw the face area to extend from the finger tip to the first knuckle. To "dress" the finger puppet use felt tip marking pens and decorate the entire finger to where it joins the hand. Polka dots are a simple dress. Try a bow tie with a striped or plaid shirt.

Nursery rhymes and simple songs work well for these puppets.

Fist Puppet
MATERIALS:

Black non-toxic, water soluble felt tip marking pen
Cellophane tape
Red lipstick
Scarf or hair ribbon

Directions: Make the left hand into a fist by tucking the thumb under the fingers. Use lipstick to outline a mouth at the opening created where the thumb meets the fingers. Tilt the hand slightly. Draw eyebrows and eyes on the upper part of the fist. Wrap the fist in the scarf, to look like a "little face" peeking from under a headscarf. Or instead of wrapping the fist, make a bow and tape it on top of the fist as a hair ribbon or attach with the tape under the mouth for a bow necktie.

Move the thumb around, up and down, sideways to make the fist puppet alive and talking.

Dancing Finger Puppets

The second and third fingers on one hand are the legs for this puppet.
MATERIALS:

Crayons or non-toxic felt tip marking pens

Paper doll figure, or self-drawn figure
Paper glue
Poster board
Scissors
Thick rubber band

Directions: Create the figure without legs. If making a girl, have a full skirt, a boy would have shorts not long pants. Color and cut out the figure. Trace the figure outline on to poster board and cut out the blank posterboard figure. Staple a rubber band in two places on the back of the poster board figure. The rubber band will serve as the holding device to keep the puppet on the fingers.

Glue the picture to its blank posterboard shape. Waiting to glue the picture until after the stapling will hide the staples. Slip fingers through the rubberband and watch the puppet dance as you wiggle your fingers.

Instant Fabric Finger Puppets
MATERIALS:

Men's white work glove
Felt tip marking pen
White craft glue
Yarn
Scissors

Directions: Cut the fingers out of the clean glove. Put faces on the loose fabric fingers. Adorn by gluing on hair and whatever else is desired by the artist.

Fabric Finger Puppets
MATERIALS:

Felt
Pencil
Felt tip marking pen (fine line)
Yarn, sequins etc.
Fabric glue
Pinking shears

Directions: Fold the felt once for double thickness. Put your pointer finger on the felt and draw around it allowing an extra half inch all around. With the pinking shears cut on the line. Dot glue around the border of one shape, leaving space at the bottom to insert the finger.

Place the second shape on top so that the pinked edges are lined up point by point. Put a book or heavy weight on the puppet for a few minutes to keep the felt flat as the glue sets up. Adorn the puppet with felt pen or sequin eyes, yarn hair, lace collar, hat etc.

Hint: Frizzed out brown twine makes interesting hair.

Variation: To have a smooth seam, place right sides of the fabric together and using a sewing machine stitch instead of gluing the edges. After stitching is completed, turn the puppet right side out and decorate.

Paper Hats For Felt Finger Puppets

Halloween Witch's Hat: Cut two 2-inch circles from black construction paper. Remove the center from one circle. It will look like a ring. This is the brim of the hat. Cut the second circle in half. Roll one half so it looks like a cone. Glue or tape the cone together. Cut five small slits around the bottom of the cone. Slide the brim over the cone, fold the tabs under the brim, then glue them to the under portion of the brim.

Mexican Hats: Follow the cutting directions for the witch's hat using yellow paper and decorate with red felt tip marking pen for a Pancho Villa sombrero. Use black paper and decorate the brim with white string for The Cisco Kid or Zorro.

Robin Hood Hat: Fold a tiny paper hat from green construction paper. Add a small feather for decoration.

Abe Lincoln Stovepipe Hat: Cut a rectangle and a circle out of black paper. Cut flaps in the bottom of one end the rectangle. Cut out the center of the circle to make a ring. Roll the rectangle into a cylinder and glue. Slip the cylinder through the center of the circle and glue the flaps under the brim to hold the pieces together.

Leprechaun's Hat: Follow the directions for making the stovepipe hat using green paper. Cut a tiny white shamrock to glue onto the front of the hat.

Glove Puppet

Although it resembles a mitten rather than a glove, this puppet is manipulated by a hand inserted into the "glove style" body.

MATERIALS:
2 8" X 12" squares of solid color fabric
Felt tip marking pens
Needle and thread
Straight pins
Pinking shears
Yarn, buttons, sequins etc.

Directions: Place the fabric squares with the right sides together, one on top of the other and pin to hold together. Position one hand with fingers together and thumb extended on the upper two-thirds area of fabric. Beginning on the inside of the wrist area, trace around the hand above the fingertips ending at the outer wrist area. The line should be approximately 1/2-inch away from the hand all the way around. This is the stitching line.

Draw a second line about 1/2-inch away from the first line. Use the outer second line as your cutting guide. Cut out the puppet. By hand or on a sewing machine stitch around the puppet using the line as a guide. Pin the pieces if necessary to hold them together while stitching. Turn the puppet right side out. For a puppet to be used by a small child, design the features with felt tip markers. Older children enjoy creating facial features for their puppets from buttons, sequins and other small items securely sewn or glued.

Sew strands or loops of yarn for hair. If using solid color fabric, make decorative designs on the cloth with felt tip marking pens. Ruffles, sequins, etc. can be added.

Hint: As the hand is traced on the fabric, leave plenty of fabric in "sleeve" fashion to conceal as much of the arm as possible. The more sophisticated the artist, the more detailed the puppet. An older child may want a "two arm" puppet. This requires using the thumb and little finger to create the arms. The simple glove puppet described above has one arm (the thumb) but may easily be converted by extending the little finger and drawing around it as well as the thumb.

Wooden Spoon Puppet
What an opportunity to show how two-faced a puppet can be! Actually a wooden spoon base makes a versatile puppet. Both sides of the spoon are suitable face surfaces. Perhaps a puppet has a happy side and a gloomy side. With a flip of the spoon the artist may create two distinctive puppet people, mother and father, mother and daughter, brother and sister, teacher and pupil.

MATERIALS:
Construction paper
Cotton balls
Model paints and brushes
Print fabric
Sandpaper (optional)
Scissors
Tape
Wooden spoon

General Directions: Check the front and back of the spoon for rough spots. Sand if necessary for a completely smooth surface. Paint a big, bold face on the back of the spoon. If you plan to have a reversible puppet you could have one side smiling and the other side frowning, or perhaps a sleeping side and an awake side.

A Clown: Paint clown features for the face. For the clown's hair, pull four cotton balls, gently spreading them. Arrange and glue for the hair. For the clown's costume, cut an 18-inch circle of fabric (polka dot, stripe, etc.) and make a very small hole in the center of the cloth. Cut five 3-inch diameter circles from construction paper. Poke a hole in the center of each paper circle, and slide the circles up the spoon handle to the head. Poke the handle through the fabric and bring the fabric up to the construction paper collar. Reach under the fabric and tape the costume to the handle.

Hint: Clown collars may be made from fabric cut with pinking shears, gathered and glued to neck. Also try pre-gathered lacy ruffles for collar decoration.

A Sweet Little Girl: Braid several strands of rug yarn and tie at both ends and in the middle. Glue the yarn at the middle tie to the top of the head. Let the braids hang down either side of the face. Wrap a length of lace two or three times around the neck and glue into position before adding the dress.

A Bad Guy: With a broad tip black felt tip marking pen, color the spoon handle black. Next, with the same marker dab at a piece of cotton until it turns dingy gray/black. Glue it on the head creating a wild look. Accentuate the eyebrows with black yarn. Make a little fringed yarn goatee. Create a cape by gathering a 5- X 8-inch strip of fabric around the "neck" and tying it with black yarn.

The Good Fairy: Paint delicate, happy features. Make hair by gluing spanish moss, or finely pulled and separated brown twine. Cut an 18-inch circle of white fabric and make a tiny hole in the center of the circle. Cut a 16-inch circle of white or pastel tulle or organdy and make a tiny hole in the center of the circle.

Slip the organdy circle up the handle and then the solid white. Gather the fabrics and apply a very small amount of glue to hold the fabrics in place on the spoon handle. Tie thin satin ribbon or yarn around the neck making sure to leave 1/4- to 1/2-inch of fabric for a ruffle.

Glue little stars, sequins, pearls etc. on the "gown."

Paper Plate Puppets
MATERIALS:
Construction paper
Fabric cut in a 14" X 14" square
Felt tip marking pens (broad and fine tip)
White craft glue
Pencil
Ruler or painter's stir stick
Scissors
Tape
White paper plate

Directions: Decide the type of face needed and with the felt tip marking pens, create a face on the convex (rounded out) side of the paper plate. For hair, mustaches, eyebrows use fuzzy fake fur fabric, cotton balls or yarn.

To make curly hair, cut strips of construction paper and wind them around a pencil then glue to paper plate. For long, springy curls use curling ribbon. Tape the ruler securely to the back of the plate. Make a small slit in the center of the fabric square, just large enough for the ruler to pass through. Slide the fabric up the ruler, so it stops behind the plate. Tape the fabric securely to the stick. The fabric hides the ruler-holding hand and also serves as a costume.

Plate face puppets perform well from behind cloth covered table or chairback "stages."

"Stuffy," The Lunch Bag Puppet
Although many "Stuffys" were made at our kitchen table, invariably at least one bore a strong resemblance to Adolph Hitler.
MATERIALS:
Brown paper lunch bag
Cotton balls

Felt tip marking pen
Newspaper, crumpled
String and yarn

Directions: Position the brown paper bag on a flat surface with long unfolded surface up and the "bottom fold side" down. Draw eyes, nose, and mouth on the top third of the bag. Open the bag and stuff it about half full with crumpled newspaper.

Tie a string under the stuffed head to make a neck. Pull cotton to make wispy hair. Glue yarn or twine to the head for hair, eyebrows, and mustache. Using felt tip marking pens, stickers, bits of paper etc. decorate the "body" of the bag with stripes, polka dots, plaids etc.

Not only should the neck string be tied to allow room for a finger to slip through, but also space should be provided in the stuffed area to stick the second or third finger (which ever is the most flexible) into the head. It might take some poking and rearranging of newspaper to make the finger hole.

Mark on the bag where the thumb and little finger would like to poke out, then cut holes for the fingers. The fingers will be the puppet arms.

Variation: Stuffy can be turned into an elephant by making a hole for the trunk (the forefinger) instead of arm holes. Cut an oval from another brown bag or colored (your choice) construction paper. Cut the oval in half and tape or glue on each side of the head for ears. Tie around the neck with yarn or twine.

Hanging Puppets

Although these puppets are not marionettes, they are suspended and operated from above the puppet stage rather than from under or behind the stage.

MATERIALS:

Dowel sticks (Select very thin dowels or green garden stakes. Length is determined by stage size.)
Felt tip marking pens
Large index cards or poster board
Paper clips
Scissors
Tape

Directions: Draw figures to be used for puppets (people, animals, super heroes, and bad guys etc.) Consider using sturdy paper dolls too.

If the paper doll is floppy, reinforce with posterboard backing.

It is easier to color the front and back of each figure before cutting. Tape a stick securely to the back of each figure so the puppet is at the bottom and the stick stretches up. Open a paper clip and bend it so it forms a large hook. Tape this hook near the top of the stick. The hook can be used to hang the puppet in a stationary position so if the play dictates, he may remain "on stage" while other puppets are in motion.

To create a pop-up puppet worked from beneath the stage, tape the figure to the top of the stick so the stick extends down. Eliminate the hook.

Variation: Tape a reinforced paper doll so that it stands on the flat side of a ruler. The puppet looks free standing but may be moved forward, backward, or from side to side as the ruler moves.

A Paper Puppet With Flexible Arms And Legs
MATERIALS:
>Felt tip marking pens
>Hole punch
>Paper fasteners
>Pencil
>Poster board
>Scissors

Directions: Make a sketch or master plan for the general appearance of the puppet. Draw the assorted pieces of the puppet on the poster board. Pieces should include:
>Torso with head attached
>2 upper arm segments
>2 lower arm segments with hands
>2 thigh segments
>2 lower leg segments with feet attached

Extend the length of the arms and legs because they will have to overlap with the body when fastened. Cut out the pieces and use the hole punch to make holes for the joints. Decorate both sides of the puppet with the felt tip marking pens. By having a front and back the puppet can turn and move about.

Assemble the puppet, joining arms, legs and torso with paper fasteners. Tape the puppet to the bottom of a slender stick. Attach a paper clip hook as described in the Hanging Puppets section.

Puppet Stages

Easy Stage I
MATERIALS:

Table cloth, curtain or sheet

A spring curtain rod that will fit securely in a doorway.

Directions: Drape the fabric over the curtain rod.

Easy Stage II
MATERIALS:

Table cloth or other print fabric that will stretch the width of a doorway.

Masking Tape
Straight pins (4)

Directions: Determine the height that is comfortable for working the puppets. Some puppeteers kneel while others prefer to sit. Stretch the fabric at the predetermined stage height across a doorway. Very carefully use two pins in the upper right corner and two pins in the upper left corner of the fabric to hold the fabric to the woodwork. The pins hold the fabric as the masking tape is applied at 4-inch intervals down both sides of the doorway.

Use this to present glove, wooden spoon, and paper plate puppet shows.

Easy Stage III
MATERIALS:

Card table
Sheet, table cloth or extra large bath towel

Directions: Open the legs of the card table and turn the table on the side so the legs face in, creating a work area for the puppeteer. Cover the table with fabric. Puppeteers may desire privacy so drape the legs of the card table.

Variation: Position the fabric-draped card table in a doorway so the audience is in one room and the puppeteers operate in privacy from the other room.

Lap Top Stage
MATERIALS:
Shoe box
Colored construction paper
Self-adhesive paper, wallpaper scraps
Index cards
Old magazines, catalogs etc.
Scissors
Paper Glue

Directions: For the exterior, turn the shoebox on its side. Cover one long side and two short sides of the shoe box with colorful self-adhesive paper. Decide upon either basic scenery such as trees, a house, a fence or specific scenery needed for a particular story.

If small suitable pictures are available in magazines and catalogs, cut them out and glue to the inside back of the box for the background. For a woodland backdrop, draw trees and shrubs on sturdy note cards. Color and cut out and glue or prop against the inside walls.

With the box on its side and the opening as the front of the stage, cut several 3- to 4-inch slits along the bottom. The lap top theater with slits is used for little puppets mounted on short, thin dowel sticks, tongue depressors or craft sticks.

Balance the shoe box on your knees. Insert the stick with the puppet on it down through the slit until it looks as if the puppet is standing. Grasp the stick under the stage and ease the puppet along the slit for movement.

Theater For Suspended Puppets
MATERIALS:
Cardboard box
1/8" width dowel sticks. Length will vary according to the size of the box. (Garden stakes may be substituted.)
Felt tip marking pens
Paper clips
Pencil
Poster board
Roll of heavy weight all purpose wrapping paper (wallpaper makes a good theater covering too)
Scissors

Directions: Set the box right side up with the opening at the top.

On one side mark off and cut out the opening for the stage. Cut a flap on either side of the box to use with a high intensity lamp or a flashlight for special lighting effects.

Decorate the exterior of the theater either by covering with wrapping paper or with paint. If the theater is to have a name, write it above the stage-opening with the felt tip pens. Cover the interior back with solid color paper.

Measure along the two sides and make corresponding notches at three-inch intervals on each side. Draw, color and cut out scenery such as trees, a sun, a cave, etc. Tape the tops of the pieces of scenery securely to the dowel. Plan for a bit of overhang on each side so as the dowels are positioned in their grooves, they stick out beyond the width of the box.

Prepare hanging or suspended puppets for use in this theater.

The Granddaddy Of All Puppet Stages

Visit an appliance store, go to the service department and ask for a refrigerator box. It is a rare service department manager who can resist the request when you are escorted by an enthusiastic child with a homemade puppet.

MATERIALS:
Craft knife
Refrigerator box
Water soluble latex paint and paintbrush
Wallpaper
Ruler
Felt tip marking pen
Black or other color electrical tape
Glitter, metallic trim, gummed stars etc.
Craft glue
Fabric for curtain (amount depends upon the size of the window)
Fabric glue
Heavy twine or clothesline

Directions: Cut a large doorway in the back of the box. The entire back may be removed if desired. Leave the top, bottom and three sides for stability.

On the side opposite the door measure and mark with the felt tip marking pen a window area near the top one-third of the box. Don't mark or cut clear to the sides of the box. Leave a 4- to 6-inch border around the window as you cut.

Paint and decorate the exterior in a bright and colorful way. Use everything available to achieve the theatrical and magic "glitzy" look.

After the artists have completed the decorations, run colorful plastic tape around the window opening. This gives the stage a finished look and covers any uneven edges.

To Make The Curtain: To determine whether to cut the fabric or leave it whole, decide how the curtain should open. One piece may be pulled back to either right or left. If the curtain is to be divided in the middle, it may be pushed to both sides for the performance.

On top create a casing for the curtain string by folding over 1-inch of fabric. Run a line of glue along the bottom edge of the fold and press down to hold fabric in place. Follow the same procedure to form the hem of the curtain. Run the string through the curtain. Knot both ends of the string and determine where inside the box the curtain is to be hung. Tape the string into place.

Let's Pretend

Playing Dress-Up

Every house where children are welcome needs a dress-up bag tucked away in the hall closet. Time and again in-house tension was alleviated when one or more children consulted the dress-up bag, assuming a different persona. My daughter Jenny had to hold her own against three brothers.

When she could coerce them into dressing up, Jenny was Mrs. Winkler, the teacher, and little brothers Matt and Sandy were the students. Sometimes Mrs. Winkler took her students dressed as a striped Dr. Seuss type cat and a little professor with brief case on field trips around the block. On other days she'd call her cousin Jean who lived just up the street. The girls would huddle in Jenny's room for a while and emerge as "elegant" ladies. Off they'd go, walking around the block, stopping to pick up their friend Caroline, also in elegant dress. Frequently Caroline's big black dog, Caesar, dressed in a shirt and gym shorts escorted the "elegant ladies" to our house where they played whatever it is elegant ladies play on afternoons when they are sick of their brothers.

Assembling a dress-up bag is easy. Before you drop off those old things at a thrift shop, sort through and save a few things for the bag. Hats, scarves, gloves and old jewelry are crucial. If you have none, visit the thrift shop, garage sales, or flea markets to see what you can find. Here is a small suggestion list to get the dress-up bag under way.

The Bag

> Old eyeglass frames (without the glass)
> Man's long tee shirt or undershirt
> Man's jacket or wrap bathrobe
> Man's ball cap or other hat
> Woman's skirt or dress (elastic waist garments are the best!)
> Women's accessories such as scarves, hats, purses, gloves earrings, necklaces etc.)
> Table cloth (can become a shawl, toga or whatever)
> Old curtains (organdy or lacy look)
> Wigs, wiglets, hairpieces (Not enough can be said about how wigs etc. add to the enjoyment of dress-up. Watch the discount stores at Halloween time and pick up inexpensive wigs in a variety of colors.)

Being Musicians

I had the good fortune to grow up in a home with a musical grandfather. He acquainted and delighted me with classical music on the old "78" Victrola. As he introduced me to less lofty compositions, my grandfather bounced me on his knees and played his harmonica. He sang me songs that made my grandmother, "More Momma," frown.

Why is it children can't remember where the other shoe is or to come home on time, but they can remember the words to raunchy songs? My grandfather taught me "Old Mike Dugan," a gem of a song which tells of Saturday night visits with old Mike Dugan who had bedbugs which shinnied up his bed post in the candle light. He always sang the one about the co-ed who eats potatoes with her knife and leaves the water in the tub after her weekly bath. Oh how I loved those songs!

After the war when my Daddy came home, our house was filled

with his music. My Daddy was a whistler. He wasn't a through-your-teeth, call-the-dog whistler; he was a warbler. In the dark of winter when birds were gone, my Daddy filled the air with warbling tunes.

Neither could I play the harmonica nor could I pucker up and whistle. I had no front teeth to spit or whistle through so Daddy taught me how to make a grass whistle. True, it was not melodic, but nevertheless it was a whistle.

A Grass Whistle

Select a broad blade of grass. Crab grass is splendid. Grip the broad bottom of the blade of grass in the plump pads at the base of the thumbs. Run the grass between the thumbs so that a thin edge is exposed in the little gap between the thumbs. Into the gap is where you blow – gently, or the grass will split. The thickness of the blade of grass will determine how shrill the sound. Experiment!

Hummer Or Poor Man's Kazoo
MATERIALS:
Waxed paper
Pocket comb

Directions: Cover a pocket comb with a piece of waxed paper. Draw your lips in over your teeth, place the paper-covered tooth edge into your mouth and hum a song into the paper-covered comb.

Hint: With friends and family members form a hummer band.

Rhythm Bells
MATERIALS:
Wide waistband-style elastic
8 large sleigh bells
Scissors
Needle and thread
Safety pins

Directions: Cut two strips of elastic long enough to overlap on the wrists or ankles. Sew four bells at intervals along one side of the elastic strip. Repeat the bell stitching on the second strip of elastic. Wrap around musician's wrists or ankles and pin to fit.

Make music by stomping the feet or shaking the arms in time to the music.

Rhythm Makers
ORNAMENTAL GOURDS AS MARACAS
In the fall most grocery stores and roadside stands have decorative, ornamental gourds for sale. Use the gourds as decorations for fall. Store the gourds in a warm dry place. As the gourds dry they become almost weightless. The seeds shake loose inside and make rattling sounds.

PLASTIC TUB SHAKERS
Measure a tablespoon of unpopped corn, dried limas, dried lentils or other beans into small, medium and large margarine tubs or other plastic containers with lids. Tape the lids to prevent accidental openings. Shake as a rhythm instrument.

PAPER PLATE TAMBOURINE
Materials:
2 paper plates
2 tablespoons of unpopped corn
Craft glue
Clothes pins
Colored yarn
Scissors
Stapler
Felt tip marking pens

Directions: Spread glue around the edge of a paper plate. Put a tablespoon of unpopped corn in the center of the plate. Cut 10 strips of colored yarn in varying lengths. Place the yarn on one glued edge to hang out as a colorful tail.

Fit the second plate edge on edge with the first plate. Clip the edges with clothes pins until the glue is dry. Remove the clothes pins and staple at intervals all around the edge of the joined plates. This is for extra security. Decorate the plates in colorful designs with the felt tip marking pens. Shake the plate like a tambourine.

Charades
This ultimate imagination guessing game is fun for all ages. Cliches, phrases, proverbs, book and movie titles etc. are used.

The challenge: For one player to successfully act out a phrase, movie title, book title, etc. so his team will be able to guess what it is in the allotted time. Before you begin:

Appoint a time/scorekeeper.

Divide the players into two groups.

Directions: A representative of Group I is given the idea by Group II and tries through pantomime and a series of universal gestures to get his group to guess the correct phrase in 60 seconds.

The presenter, never saying a word, must first establish the category – book, movie, song, etc. Next, he or she must indicate how many words are involved. Then the creative imagination kicks in.

Group II, knowing the idea, watches and tries to remain silent. If Group I misses, roles are reversed. Should Group I guess correctly, other players from Group I choose and play out the charades until Group I is "Stumped." After all players on both sides have had a turn, move to the 30-second lightning round.

Scoring: One point for guessing within the 60-second limit. Two points for guessing correctly within the 30-second limit. The winner is the group with the most points at the end of the game.

Traditional Symbols For Charades

Book title: Hold hands together, palms up.

Movie title: Hold a circle made with the left thumb and forefinger up to the left eye. Make a cranking motion near the right side of the head with the right hand to emulate a movie camera.

A saying such as a motto, cliche or proverb: Make simultaneous, imaginary quotation marks in the air with second and third fingers of each hand.

Song title: Open the mouth and spread the arms as if singing.

Person: Man, point to man, for a woman point to a woman.

Sounds like: Pull the earlobe. If someone is having trouble getting the idea, sounds like will trigger rhyming words.

Stop: Hold up hand as a stop sign.

First word: Hold up one finger.

First syllable: Hold up one finger after announcement of first word.

Shorten A Word: Make a chopping motion on left forearm with right hand.

Lengthen a word: Make a stretching movement, spreading the arms.

Keep guessing: A circular motion with one hand toward the group.

Tongue Twisters

A good solid laugh is relaxing and has to be good medicine. In tense and serious times laughter is scarce. Except for nervous and inappropriate giggles, laughter seems to evaporate in the teen years as the kids sag under the weight of approaching life determining decisions. I know it does my students a world of good to lighten up and get silly once in a while.

Recently as we were preparing for a poetry unit, slogging through similes, metaphors, and personification, "it" happened. That special time teachers enjoy when students catch on, then spontaneously move ahead on their own. They took a fancy to alliterations. We had a wonderful tongue twister day. In the computer lab they typed their collection of newly composed alliterations and with imagination devised other word games to send to our "adopted" class of eight year olds.

With the students' permission I have included some of their tongue twisters to give you a chuckle and to stimulate your imagination.

Courtesy of Robby Evans
   Lately, little Louie lost lots of loot.
   Tyron the track star took tons of tomatoes _____. (your word)

Courtesy of Rashida Bassett
   Tiny Tim touched ten teasing turtles twelve times.
   Lumpy Linda laughed_____(your word) like a lion.

Courtesy of: Stacy Belch, Dayna Tillman and Cindy Williamson
   Freaky Freddy fried forty-four french fries Friday for a friend.
   Bubba blew a big blue bubble, but Bobby blew a bigger bubble.
   Kate caught creeping Kitty Cat catching _____.(your word)

Courtesy of Andrea Adams and Andrea Carver
   Raging Ross rambled rapidly about race cars.
   Tuesday tiny Tommy tripped terribly into the tub.
   Ignorant Irvin invited important individuals_____.(your word)

Hopefully, after reading this book you will now understand and are comfortable in the knowledge that it is through very simple ways that we can all make a difference in our world. No matter which road you travel, please take time along your way to revive the forgotten art of celebrating love, laughter and life with children.